Slime Dynamics

Generation, Mutation, and
the Creep of Life

Slime
Dynamics

Generation, Mutation, and
the Creep of Life

Ben Woodard

Winchester, UK
Washington, USA

First published by Zero Books, 2012
Zero Books is an imprint of John Hunt Publishing Ltd., Laurel House, Station Approach,
Alresford, Hants, SO24 9JH, UK
office1@jhpbooks.net
www.johnhuntpublishing.com
www.zero-books.net

For distributor details and how to order please visit the 'Ordering' section on our website.

ISBN: 978 1 78099 248 8

A CIP catalogue record for this book is available from the British Library.

Design: Stuart Davies

Printed and bound by CPI Group (UK) Ltd, Croydon, CR0 4YY

We operate a distinctive and ethical publishing philosophy in all
areas of our business, from our global network of authors to
production and worldwide distribution.

CONTENTS

Introduction - Slime Ascent   1

1 - The Nightmarish Microbial   14

1.2 - Fungoid Horror and The Creep of Life   26

1.3 - Extra-Galactic Terror   40

Conclusion - Slime Metaphysics?   53

Notes   69

Slime Ascent

"As long as humankind recklessly proceeds in the fateful delusion of being biologically fated for triumph, nothing essential will change."
-Peter Wessel Zapffe, *The Last Messiah*

"Life is not even meaningless."
-Herman Tønnessen, "Happiness is for the Pigs"

Millions of years ago, above a recently hardened earth, gases in the atmosphere reduced and then were exposed to solar and other forms of energy, allowing the creation of organic compounds such as nucleic and amino acids, which would eventually interact leading to the first forms of life. These globs of swarming proto-life within the primeval oceans "regulated by principles of physics for self-organizing systems" provided the template for all organic being and all eventual thought on the planet Earth.[1]

Despite the fact that humans gradually ascended from these clustered ponds of ooze, *slime*, as both a general name for a life-generative and semi-solid substance in the physical sense and the disgust of life, the ostensible grossness of organic being in a metaphysical sense, slime remains something to be left behind and forgotten. This is despite the fact that humans are well aware of the fact that our individual biological geneses consist of the unceremonious mixture of slimy biological components (of sperm and egg); sexual procreation being an obvious example of the disgusting yet generative articulation of slime-as-life and life-as-slime.

While it would be impossible to exhaustively explore the numerous religious and cultural vestiges it can be argued that both religious and cultural discourse assert that either we are not slimy or, if we are, we can escape our sliminess through culture, aesthetics, juridical systems, piety, abstinence, or the next life if need be.

The part of this abandonment of slime we will explore results from a misconstrued sense of evolution: the sense that our sliminess can simply be shed over time, evolution as perpetual betterment instead of local adaptation. As Stephen Jay Gould describes "The vaunted progress of life is really *random motion away from simple beginnings,* not *directed impetus toward inherently advantageous complexity.*"[2] An assumption of eventual perfection attempts to rid human being of not only an accidental beginning but of its base material nature.

While the cultural and religious resistances would clearly obstruct any assertion that our existence as a species is only material and accidental, what is surprising is that intellectual adventures which set out to be more rational such as science and philosophy are themselves guilty of refusing to accept the tenuous and material moorings of humanity. That is, regardless of scientific or other intellectual discoveries it seems that humans must, for the sake of pride or simply life-justification, retain an inherent meaningfulness.

The question of life's meaning leads us to the problem of what about life makes it life? This opens up the problem of emergence—what is it exactly that is emerging from the slime pools? Emergence can be defined as the arising or generation of complex entities or systems from less complex sub systems or less complex entities. Or, put more directly, emergence allows a thing to be more than the sum of its parts. That is, at some point inorganic entities combine (under very specific environmental conditions) to create organic systems which then interact and become life. Eventually we go from chemical compounds to something like a virus (self replicating but often not considered alive) to life as a self contained, self replicating entity which grows and changes by borrowing energy from its environment. Emergence is the theoretical explanation of these jumps. Emergence is generally divided into weak emergence and strong emergence. Weak emergence implies that the novelty or change observed can be traced to the specific results of its component parts. An example of weak emergence would be explaining the structure of a snow ball from the structure of a snow flake given atmospheric changes over time. There is nothing seemingly new about the snow ball given what we know about snow, it is merely an arrangement of smaller parts into something larger. Weak emergence means that new properties arise in a physical system are reducible to the components of that system.

Strong emergence on the other hand suggests a certain irreducibility arising from a system's components. The primary example here would be consciousness or even life itself.

That is, an emergent account of consciousness would argue that consciousness arose from the work of synapses and neurons but would assert, contrary to what reductionists claim, that consciousness is essentially beyond the material capacities of neurophysiology. Strong emergence would hold that thought, on some level, escapes the limits of its physical components.

At first glance, the concept of strong emergence appears as one of the last (and strongest) bastions of anthropocentricism, of demanding that humanity deserves, or automatically occupies, a place of metaphysical or spiritual importance. Rather the issue is treating phenomenon on their own level, that is, explaining a process of digestion chemically does not explain the activity of an animal acting in order to consume food.[3]

Engaging with levels of existence can easily lead back to a formulation of existence where humanity reigns on high, if for no metaphysical reason, then for our technological or artistic capacity.

It should come as no surprise that even after the numerous dethronings of Man: Copernicus knocking us out of the center of the universe (in the heliocentric model of the solar system), Darwin kicking us face first into the pointless chance of evolution and of Freud unthreading the rationality of our own minds that humanity still attempts to remain resolutely immune to the baseness reality of life and matter.

Steven Johnson's text *Emergence* begins with Toshiyuki Nakagaki's work on slime molds in which he trained one of the blob-like creatures to find the most efficient path through a maze towards a food source despite the gooey organism's lack of cognitive function.[4] As Johnson points out, slime molds have attracted much attention since they function as both individual cells and multi-cellular organisms.[5] Slime mould behavior questions the very division between life component and life as such especially when they appear to act with intent, when they get better and better at solving the maze.

For humans, the mindless functioning of life, of organisms moving towards goals without any form of intelligence, of creatures that function in a completely bottom up fashion reasserts not only the accidence of thought but also thought's unimportance for survival. In other words, the very idea that simplistic forms of life can accomplish what seems to us complex behaviors raises the question: to what degree is higher intelligence a significant advantage? That is, the idea of complex behavior without an intelligence guiding it is ostensibly disheartening in that chance and coincidence surpass telos and destiny and yet, at the same time, if emergence is essentially pattern recognition the question becomes whether emergence is merely an objective or subjective category. Does emergence merely describe shifting patterns of complexity that only appear to us as new or does emergence make a difference in the world, in an ontological or at least non-sensorial way?

In regards to biology emergence suggests a non-intentional

behavior or set of behaviors between already constituted objects. Take for example ants in an ant colony which we know as individual organisms and observe as a swarm of ants. A swarm is a pattern that necessitates an empirically decided boundary be placed on the moving object (that is, what counts as a part must be decided). A swarm must be a swarm of something. A swarm's behavior is a result of the actions of the individual things in relation to its proximity to other individuals. A flock of birds for instance occurs not because of any centralized coordination but because the birds follow individual needs in the vicinity of others birds benefiting themselves and one another. While in collective animal behavior it is easy to distinguish the components of the swam or flock, the ability to tell object from non-object centers on the divide between weak (or epistemological emergence) and strong (or ontological emergence).

In physics, for instance, it is a matter of debate whether sub-atomic particles can be described as objects or whether they are merely points or zero dimensional objects. But is a point, or zero-dimensional object, different from the name of the thing itself as a point? That is, when do we know when have arrived at the fundamental part of any human-defined thing or object or body?

To return to the question of life and its creation, is life ontologically emergent or is it an identity and not a fact since we cannot say why life emerges but only that once a life emerges (and is classified as human, monkey, etc.) we can then distinguish its identifiable existence from its components. We must question then what kind of differences are 'real' or what is it about particular species that have real effects versus patterns which only group movements via categories. In other words, the identity of life must be decided, as well as that of un-life.

As Jack Cohen and Iain Stewart (mathematician and biologist respectively) point out in their text *Collapse of Chaos*, the difficulty lies in discovering the complexity of simplicity. Emergence is commonly opposed to reductionism, to the theory that phenomena can be explained by its lesser components that "a collection of interacting components can 'spontaneously' develop collective properties that seem not to be implicit in any way in the individual pieces."[6] Cohen and Stewart point out however that without knowing what is meant by simplicity, by simple components, emergence means very little. Cohen and Stewart acknowledge that humans tend to create patterns by smoothing out fluctuations in their observable world[7] and that patterns are after all ideals.[8]

On the other hand reductionism explains the how but not the why of life since it does not take into account the resulting feedback effects of externality on the development of life. As an example Cohen and Stewart compare the eyes of herbivores to those of carnivores. They argue that where a reductionist explanation would tell us how the eyes developed via DNA and biochemistry it would not explain that evolutionarily herbivores with eyes at the side of their head to watch for predators thrived as did carnivores with eyes that faced forward and therefore were useful for hunting.[9]

On a large scale Cohen and Stewart point out that evolution and emergence have created a landscape where space and competing species create bottlenecks and bridges that lead to convergence overriding contingency in differing eco-spaces.[10] The conclusions that Cohen and Stewart draw from these arguments lead to assertions about humans that seem to lean towards a form of anthrocentrism. They write: "The patterns that our brains perceive are accurate representations of large chunks of reality because our brains and sense organs evolved that way."[11] This argument seems to shed the haphazard nature of human evolution in that it assumes that convergence overrides the contingent factors of evolution. That is, the jump between animals having strategically oriented eyes and humans having a brain that can understand, even indirectly, the deep structures of the universe, seems somewhat dubious. Ray Brassier, whose work we will engage heavily towards the end of this text comments on this problem albeit in a philosophical context: "The chief obstacle standing in the way of a proper scientific understanding of the physical world would seem to be that of our species' inbuilt tendency to process information via epistemic mechanisms which invariably involve an operation of subtraction from the imperceptible physical whole."[12] In other words, human knowledge obtained through observation tends to be contoured by the fact that we think and observe according to our own perceptible world and concerns.

To return to biology, Gary Marcus makes clear in his text *Kluge*, that the human brain is only a slapped together piece of faulty machinery, where adaptation and development are a response to threats more than anything and that our minds are always built upon pre-existing structures.[13] For Cohen and Stewart convergence points towards deeper structures since those structures influence convergence for Marcus and others, context just as easily leads our brains away from any deeper understanding of the universe towards quick and dirty survival tactics meant for the short term.

The issue then becomes one of navigating reductionism, mechanism, and emergence without lapsing into anthropic assertions about the nature of the universe or unrealistically cheer-leading our own epistemic capacities. While we could agree that the mind is caused by but cannot be derived from fine structures and rules this fact does not trump those fine structures.[14] We cannot say that emergence is ontological in regards to life but only that it is epistemological.[15] The question is how do we divide our mental capacities from the reality of the universe – or how naturally in tune with the universe is conscious thought, or is it ever?

At this point it becomes necessary (or at least prudent) to step from science to philosophy and define the general philosophical approach of the following text as aligned with the emerging movement of Speculative Realism. Speculative Realism names a collection of disparate alternatives to the dominance of what Quentin Meillassoux names correlationism. Correlationism is the assertion that there must be a reciprocal relation between thinking and what is thought, that "there can be no cognizable reality independently of our relation to reality."[16]

The anti-correlationist, what we could also call anti-anthropocentric, assertion we will make here is one following Iain Hamilton Grant (one of the original four Speculative Realist thinkers along with Ray Brassier, Graham Harman and the recently mentioned Meillassoux) stating that something must exist prior to thinking and that something is nature.[17] In a seemingly backwards move in regards to the question of life, the approach to thinking this nature will be one of vitalism not as centering on an enigmatic life-force but as centering on, discovering and, understanding the forces which operate on and within life. Vitalism provides a formalization of our ignorance and perhaps a fundamental gap or inability to completely grasp the Real, the actual deep reality of the universe, of ourselves, of what we call nature and our placement within it.

As the guiding theme of this text, I propose an odd metaphysical construct opposed to emergence and that is at once a simultaneous resurrection and mutilation of vitalism. Traditionally vitalism does not seem too different from emergentism in that both suggest there is something more to life, something that drives and/or affects life that is not purely reducible to the classifiable components of life itself. The two have been grouped together by critics and proponents alike.

The vitalism we will be pursuing here avoids this connect in that it is not a theory that asserts a vital substance or stuff that propels life forward, but that the vital force is time and its effect on space. This at first may seem not like a vitalism at all but the focus of this project is to prove the effects of the temporal-spatial construction of existence on life as not merely the force of, but a force acting upon life that provides a rigorously deanthropomo-prhizing way of thinking. We will show that accounting for time and space does not undo vitalism but pushes it to its logical philosophical conclusion.

The contemporary philosophical orientation of vitalism is most associated with the work of Gilles Deleuze and Felix Guattari and it is against their use of the term that we must first set out to introduce our own spatio-temporal version outlined above. In *What is Philosophy?* Deleuze and Guattari describe vitalism as split between an "Idea that acts but is not and a force that is but does not act."[18]

In the first half of Deleuze and Guattari's damnation of vitalism, vitalism is merely a guiding concept without any sort of material consequence. In the second half it has a material substance but one that has no discernible impact. Deleuze and Guattari's attack can be traced to a comment by the French thinker Henry Bergson who in his text *Creative Evolution* notes that vitalism adds nothing to change or to the emergence of life since life's stages can be described by heredity. The French phenomenologist Maurice Merleau-Ponty in his lectures on nature added and expanded on Bergson's account pointing out that one glaring issue with vitalism is its disregard of space – that it is assumed that some lively (but non-physical) substance (an élan vital) was moved across space, that it affected organisms without any concern for the spatial restraints of biological reality.

Summed up, for Deleuze, Guattari, Bergson and Merleau-Ponty, vitalism cannot be a thing (since genes are what is passed on, not life itself) and it cannot be a force because it says nothing about life itself as a force, only that it develops but not how. What all the aforementioned critiques leave out is time as something beyond thought which is the force of vitalism (life emerges over time) and the substance of vitalism is not the germ plasm trumping heredity but space as it is filled by life. A spatial-ization of vitalism simply points to the fact that an organism attempts to extend itself across space through growth, mutation, and reproduction. A temporalization of vitalism likewise can be seen as the fact that life happens with time and that time means the birth as well as the death of all things.

H.P. Lovecraft, whose fiction will occupy much of the third chapter, was also disdainful of vitalism, placing it somewhere between the mythical and the poetic.[19] This was mostly due to the vital force being taken as essentially spiritual and not energetic, as a fundamentally non-scientific vitalism thereby opposing Lovecraft's own adamant espousal of mechanism and determinism.

Finally the aforementioned construction of vitalism can be taken as a response to one more strike against vitalism from the naturephilosopher F.W.J. Schelling, who commented that a force of nature (vitalism) is a self contradictory concept in that a force must be opposed, or in relative equilibrium, or in perpetual conflict, arguing that vitalism met none of these criteria.[20] Since space and time work together and upon one another we can therefore claim that this formulation of vitalism passes Schelling's rigorous rubric.

How do we further explicate vitalism, bring it into contact with reality and raise it from its spatio-temporal philosophical obscurity? Vitalism, as it has been articulated here, is a minimalist metaphysics which operates on reality by way of following an ontological cascade mirroring the cosmological progression of forces and matters. At the root of this vitalism is the force of forces following from an original One, a One not as a pure unification but the possibility of 'isness' itself stemming from the original simultaneous explosion of time and space as well as the resulting emanations, immanences, emergences and transcendences.

That is, vitalism is a mental shadow of the progression of the universe, from the speculative moment before the Big Bang, as a highly condensed mass, to its extension into time and space and matter, to biological life, and finally to reflective thinking. The above mentioned ontological cascade moves (in philosophical terms) from the Real, to Materiality, to Sense, and finally to Extilligence. Or, put in terms of the levels of the reality it mirrors, from bare existence as only possibility, to the configurations of matter and energy, to the interaction of stimulus and sense, ending with the extension of ontic being via symbols, structures, technologies, et cetera. The degenerate take on vitalism and the Neo-Platonic One will be taken together as a dark vitalism. But what is it about this conceptualization of vitalism that makes it dark exactly?

Part of the work of a dark vitalism is the sickening realization of an inhospitable universe, stating that the production of life as an accidental event in time which is then contorted and bent by the banality of space, of our particular (and just as accidental) universal geometry and then further ravaged by accident, context, feedback and the degradation of wear and age.

The dark of dark vitalism is thus three fold:

1 – It is dark because it is obscured both by nature (who is to say that we can divine and comprehend the details of the universe from our limited brains) and by time (we are at a temporal disadvantage in trying to discern the creation of all things) since the cause of most of the nature we know has fallen back into the deep past.

2 – It is dark because it spells bad news for the human race in terms of our origin (we are just clever monkeys that emerged as a result of a series of biological and cosmo-logical lucky breaks), our meaning (we are just meat puppets based on our construction), and our ultimate fate (Earth will die and we will probably perish if not with it then eventually with the universe).

3 – It is dark on an aesthetic and experiential level our psychological and phenomenological existence is

darkened and less friendly to us, and to our perceptions, given the destructiveness of time and space.

It is the third claim which this text will work hardest to prove focusing primarily on biological sciences and biological examples within popular culture through a collection of lurid cultural artifacts.

The first chapter engages the internality of dark vitalism through the unseen and unsettling interior productivity of life through mitochondria, bacteria, contagion and the like. I explore films such as *Outbreak*, survival horror games (*Deadspace, Resident Evil, Parasite Eve*) and real life examples of viruses to illustrate the terrifying interiority of the microscopic sliminess of human beings. I discuss how this relates to the question of immanence and emergence following Cohen and Stewart's *Collapse of Chaos* and Keith Ansell Pearson's biophilosophy.

I move from the interior to the exterior, looking at the spatial creep of fungoid life discussing various works of weird fiction by Thomas Ligotti, Willliam Hope Hodgson and Stanley Weinbaum to demonstrate the unnerving spatiality of molds and fungus. I will discuss Reza Negarestani's thoughts on decay and rot and argue against Michel Henry's phenomenological and human privileging conceptualization of life.

In the third chapter I argue against Gaia-inspired theories of the earth and how the generative functions of life are restricted by anthropism. I look at the unrestricted organicism of science fictive monsters (the Zerg, Species 8472, the Tyranids and Yuuzhan Vong) as well as H.P. Lovecraft's Old Ones in order to demonstrate the interspatial horror of the organic. In this section I will focus on Schelling Iain Grant's text on him.

I conclude with a discussion of Freud's Vesicle, Lacan's Lamella and Iain Grant's "Being and Slime" as describing the relation of slime to thought calling for an extension of Negarestani's Cthuluoid ethics and Brassier's conclusion of *Nihil*

Unbound in which he calls for a cosmological extension of the death drive.

The following text aims to be less about slime itself than bout the sliminess of life, of the inevitable biological and physical constraints on living in a world that, in one way or another, is always a being-towards-extinction. Slime itself, as we have seen, is always a toss a part of life meant to be left behind There has always been an attempt to externalize ooze and slime and sludge but this effort cannot grasp nor undo the sliminess of slime as internal to life itself. This project is instead a vitiation of any orderly conceptualization of life; it is a celebration and liberation of slime in all its disgusting flows.

I

The Nightmarish Microbial

"[Diseases] crucify the soul of man, attenuate our bodies, dry
them, wither them, shrivel them up like old apples, make them
as so many anatomies."
-Robert Burton, *Anatomy of Melancholy*

"Disease is the retribution of outraged Nature."
-Hosea Ballou

In his essay "The Evolution of Life on Earth" Stephen Jay Gould
takes issue with the popular delusion that life advances from one
dominant form to another, from bacteria to invertebrates, to
reptiles et cetera, eventually 'ending' or peaking in the human
organism.[21] Gould points out that we will never escape the age of
bacteria, we are only an accidental outgrowth as a result of
episodic and pointless addition.[22]

He goes on to say "Our impression that life evolves toward
greater complexity is probably a bias inspired by parochial focus
on ourselves, and consequent overattention to complexifying
creatures, while we ignore just as many lineages adapting equally
well by becoming simpler in form."[23] Gould's point is essentially
that complexity does not imply evolutionary success. Despite our
intellectual advantages it is the minuscule that has biological
dominion over the earth not only in the exteriorized microorganic nature (the world out there) but also as that which
comprises our own human interiors in terms of the molecular,
cellular, and the micro-organic. In the following chapter my aim
is to explore the tiniest forms of life and how their behavior alone
and across networks (biological and non biological) run counter

to a philosophically positive articulation of life.

To begin, mitochondria, which are often referred to as the power plants of cells, are small organelles (parts of the cell) which generate the chemical fuel needed for a cell's activities. Mitochondria have much in common with prokaryeotes, organisms such as bacteria which lack nuclei in their cells. The somewhat alien nature of organelles has led to the development of the endosymbiotic theory which asserts that organelles were, at one point, separate organisms that were later incorporated into cells. The separate organisms made the eventual transition from a cooperative network to an integrated cell.

The symbiotic is only one step away from the parasitic, a closeness explored via the parasitic and violent potential of mitochondria in Hideaki Senai's novel, and the subsequent game series, *Parasite Eve*. Senai makes the odd jump of saying that mitochondria form a kind of super organism (something we will address further on) and that with their generative capacity can cause spontaneous combustion. Nick Land elaborates: "The difference between parasitism and symbiosis is very slippery [...] Merely contributing to stability can be construed as a cooperative function, whilst at the other pole the recent movie *Parasite Eve* anticipates a mitochondrial insurgency – triggered at a threshold of biomolecular science – that unmasks the 'symbiotic' mitochondria as strategic parasites."[24] The most interesting aspect of *Parasite Eve* is that it points (albeit hyperbolically) to the fact that the destructive capacity of life's smallest components are indissociable from its generative capability.

Given the competitive violence of life's productivity it seems ridiculous to assume that there would be any sort of deep down harmony between life forms (whether psychic or not) across the globe as all creatures are all battling for limited space and resources in their individual biospheres. The interconnectedness of various life forms on the earth is a tenuous intermeshing based on opportunity and luck and not due to any artificially imposed harmony. From the disrupted familiarity of mitochondria we move to the more externalized, (at least in terms of the biological boundaries of the human, of our normal functioning) yet still internal virus to explore the horror of the network and of internality, the virus being an object which pushes the nightmarish capacity of networked life to its limits.

The virus, the viroid, the deadly bacterium, all crept into center stage prior to the turn of the twentieth to the twentieth first century. The vague swarming of the deadly microbial and the subsequent paranoia emerged alongside the rise of a globalized and interconnected world, where proximity and speed elevated the potency and spread of contagion. The political correlative to this is that the dissemination of nation states and rise of globalization exacerbated worries over security, of the permeability of one's borders. That is, while the microbial raises worries of internal biological damage, fears of the viral place human beings in a biological ecology full of unfriendly entities.

Media episodes of epidemic outbreak point to the magnitude of viral voraciousness but often only indirectly as the real object in the spotlight is the capacities of governmental infrastructure, what is being done or not done, to respond to the biological threat. Thus the attention is shifted from the potential horror of viewing the collective biomass of the human race as only viral food, to the demands of our external capabilities found in technology government and reason. Endless speculative scenarios have paraded across various fictional stages exemplifying the apocalyptic capacities of infection: *The Scarlet Plague, The Masque of the Red Death, The Andromeda Strain, 28 Days Later, Cabin Fever* et cetera. Such mental exercises however do little justice to the realities of AIDS, Tuberculosis, Malaria, and Influenza to only name a few forms of viral life which consistently evade eradication.

This interconnected disease-space meant a further stretching and clandestine malformation of militarization, of military forces as themselves moving like small swarms undetected and largely unseen. The two, the rampancy of the viral and the partial openness of globalization, meet in the schizoid possibility (and reality) of bio-weapons development illustrated finely in Wolfgang Petersen's epidemological sci-fi film *Outbreak*.

In the opening scene of *Outbreak*, a small village is fire bombed to contain the spread of a fictional filvirade virus called Motaba which acts like Ebola and Marburgh, replicating at a rapid speed and liquefying the insides of the victims. It soon becomes clear that the bomb did not contain the virus and that the colossal systems of the military are ill equipped to contain the virus on the whole. But instead of adapting to contain the virus the military only wishes to sample and produce the disease as a viral weapon thereby redirecting the destruction of the virus rather than containing or eradicating it. The interesting aspect here is that the virus is faulty confronted (by the military) as a form of death and treated as a form of life by the doctors who ultimately save the day. In other words, the virus and the infected bodies are collapsed in military thinking whereas they are fundamental separate in medical thinking. It is merely destructible on the one hand while curable on the other.

To return to the theme of networks which began our engagement with the viral, the closing of networks can produce results as strange and unpredictable as opening them. During the Great Plague of England the small town of Eyam quarantined itself in order to stop or at least slow the spread of the Bubonic Plague. The strategy cost the inhabitants of Eyam more than half of their population but as it now turns out, the survivors of the plague may have passed a genetic mutation onto their kin which may prove immune to other deadly contemporary contagions. As Reza Negarestani notes in his incomparable text *Cyclonopedia*, radical openness to other forms of life (viral or otherwise) can begin not with an attitude of openness but with radical closure, that one can be radically open by making oneself a target from the outside paradoxically through isolation.[25] This radical or epidemic openness exists at the cost of economic openness (of being open to a controllable degree) thereby necessitating the destruction of any clean concept of survival.[26] As Negarestani points out survival is not a given following the advent of life but is "intrinsically impossible."[27]

Microbial life becomes an interiorizing network that does not slow or cease in the face of survival but continually bores into and simultaneously in the name of life. The microbial is then perhaps a particularly insidious example of a Latourian hybrid. As Graham Harman points out via Latour, the attempt at discerning a hybrid (that is, an object comprised of both the natural and cultural) is the work of tracing the contours of a network.[28] Or in other words, Latour forgoes the explanatory fictions of the natural and the cultural preferring to ascertain the nature of an object through its relations to other entities.

This horror is found in the physical framework of the virus itself. The curable/destructable confusion and the network obfuscation of virus transmission meet yet another ambiguity – one which is within the virus itself. Debate still continues over whether viruses are organic compounds (components of life) or forms of life themselves. One can think back to our ant colony and the ambiguity between part and whole. While viruses contain RNA or DNA they are not made of cells and replicate only by hijacking cells of organisms to spread themselves.

Where the qualification of life may be difficult to place on the virus' squirmy chained body, the event of disease is, as Eugene Thacker points out, even more complex as it functions on the macro level as an assemblage of living forms such as in the case of the Black Death, "bacillicus-flea-rat-human."[29]

From a human point of view it seems unsettling to see viruses as another form of life (or even an aggregate of life-like components) as opposed to a particular materialization of death particularly as viruses are something that regularly skirt the perimeter of humanity's technological prowess—technology being that which we use to safeguard ourselves from a nature supposedly separate from us and thus theoretically controllable and understandable. Viruses serve as an uncomfortable reminder of how tenuous our so-called dominion over nature turns out to be. The microbial is not only a terrifying means of death (given its invisible nature) but also a killing of death itself, in the putrid obfuscation of contagion.

Contagion becomes neither death nor life but protracted life, a state of never quite being dead – an undeadness not of the living dead but of dead living. In his "Death as a Perversion" Negarestani speaks of an "epidemic openness" an openness that is not an open to others, a being open, but a being laid open, being splayed open to the swarming perversion of death.[30] This infected death[31] is a disterminalized death, a darker articulation of the aforementioned protracted life, death becomes cracked open and endless[32] as Victor Hugo writes in regards to a pit of slime which makes a man's death seem shapeless. Contagion forces life and death into the same generative slime.

Viral productivity and decay are both bound together by temporality as both display the horrid inward aspect of life which, as Eugene Thacker articulates in his essay "Biophilosophy for the 21st Century," spreads across borders and boundaries.[33] Thacker further elaborates in his text "Cryptobiologies" when he writes: "Microbes establish networks of infection within a body, and networks of contagion between bodies, and our modern transportation systems extend that connectivity across geopolitical borders."[34] Again, the viral exercises the networked nature between life and non-life and between part and whole under the name of contagion. The real and fantastical treatments of bio-weaponry are an indirect attempt to resolidify the messiness of disease.

Bioweaponry embraces the aforementioned split of treating contagion like death or life in that bioweaponry extends the protracted death of contagion through the body as Thacker mentions above.

In his text co-authored with Alexander Galloway, Thacker points out that naturally occurring diseases are without a cause (besides nature) whereas bioweaponary points to a creator and propagator. The concept of patient zero becomes a pivot, or half way point between an apparently malicious nature and a salacious human agent.[35] As the authors points out however, the similarity between the artificial and the natural viral outbreak is that neither one can have fully predictable consequences.[36]

Again following Thacker, contagion is paradoxical in that it demands the closure of borders and the harsh manipulation of networks, despite the fact that life itself (biologically and culturally in the human sense) is defined by borrowing energy from the environment through the openness of boundaries extended through networks. As already mentioned, the viral participates in a radical state of being open, an openness completed by the work of decayed life, decay being the spreading out and diffusion of contained or somatic life out into the biosphere as fertilizer. This decay is molded in redirected with bioweaponry. The oldest known example of bioweaponry is that of catapulting corpses into fortresses to spread disease and to smoke out the enemy with the smell of rot and the danger of miasma.[37] In his "Nine Disputations on Horror" Thacker points out that much thinking about the virus centers on the infected body not on the virus itself.[38] This corporealization reasserts the division between life and the virus, crystalizing the assumption that pathology is the inverse of life and not a part of life itself.[39]

Thacker's critique connects with the example of *Outbreak*, in that the film approaches disease in term of infected bodies and not the infection itself. That is, it is the function of protracted death extended through decay which brings the rancid openness of the viroid to its ultimate conclusion of spreading not only the disease but decay and openings beyond the limits of the body, of the corporeal. That is, the question becomes how corporeal does the viral have to be without loosening its capacity for biological opening, softening, and decaying?

To move into stranger places – the more fantastically nightmarish microbial (vampire and zombie plagues, mind controlling parasites et cetera) which is tied to science fiction and horror realms, easily suggests the temporal invasion of space by a dark vitalism through corrosive life in its tiniest forms. In this sense, even the tiniest organism embodies external forces which come from beyond what is understood in terms of nature.

The knot of competing productivity and decay is captured well in the *Resident Evil* series of games. *Resident Evil* centers on various outbreaks of bio-engineered viruses which reanimate dead tissue by replacing the once living organism's mitochondria. *Resident Evil* is the affective/aesthetic short circuit of the strain of completive life and the forces of death and decay. The fact that the game's T-Virus essentially zombifies making the dead 'living' carriers of the disease – is one step towards dematerializing or de-corporealization of the microbe, the virus and so forth.

As Thacker points out the recent variation of the game *Resident Evil Outbreak* (the first multiplayer *Resident Evil*) takes the connectivity of the virus to the connectivity of the internet.[40] The dumb blankness of an avatar gels nicely with the body to the point of death level of zombified virology, beyond this openness, in Negarestani's sense would not be representable as body.

The graphic novel and game *Dead Space* goes even further in its apt portrayal of such tiny monsters in its necromorphs – parasites which take control and zombify dead tissue – life forms that act as a disease – as an infectant – but in fact are another (conscious) life form which has no concern for the fragility of human being(s) while recognizing (unlike the virus, the microorganism) the consciousness of humans. Yet the two cannot be easily cleaved from each other. The necromorphs contort and re-flesh their victims reducing their human hosts not to zombic hunger but to a fever only to spread the protracted death of necromorph existence. Furthermore, whereas zombies are reliant on the reduced faculties of their brain pointing towards a target (removal of the head) the necromorphs must be de-limbed until they can no longer move. The strategy of combating not the center of the organism but attacking the limbs can be connected to the Jihadi strategy of dieback machinery articulated in Negarestani's article "The Militarization of Peace: Absence of Terror or Terror of Absence?"[41] The strategy of dieback which the necromorphs invoke is a self imposed withering utilizing the exteriority of the body to protect its own viral interiority. The necromorphs cannot be destroyed only their transmission vessels can be hobbled and slowed.

In regards to the philosophical consideration of contagion much has been send but it has tended towards the poetic. The metaphysical battle is to wrest the virus from its bio-politcal moors to those of bio-philosophy without falling into a philosophy of biology. Biopolitics is the means which govern-mental entities regulate, or at least attempt to regulate, all aspects of human life (and argably non-human life) where a philosophy of biology asks what is life in the most generic sense. Thacker differentiates bio-philosophy from a philosophy of biology in that the former thinks the "peripheries of life" and ontology whereas the latter attempts to think the question of what is life and epistemology.[42] Biophilosophy asserts that life equals multiplicity which, as Thacker suggests, can be taken as a renewal of vitalism a project which, is obviously important to the text at hand.[43]

Yet the specter of the rejections and denouncements of vitalism mentioned in the introduction suddenly appear in regards to the microbial. The work of Keith Ansell Pearson for instance, in allegiance to its Bergsonian and Deleuzian roots can be seen as championing (at least partially) the knowing (epistemology) and ethics of life over the being (ontology) of life particularly in regard to small forms of life.

In his text *Germinal Life*, Pearson addresses the future of biophilosophy and yet this biophilosophy is seen as what must be ethical and opposed to what he defines as two nihilisms.[44] In the opening pages of his text Pearson aligns himself in opposition to a certain "biological nihilism" when he writes that Deleuze's thought escapes "the grim law of life implicit in Weismann's theory of the germ-plasm" that would condemn 'individual' life to the eternal return of a nihilistic fate and that would dissipate the forces of the outside and minimize their influence."[45]

August Weissmann, a revolutionary biologist of the early twentieth century, advocated a germ-plasm theory which stated that hereditary information moves from genes to body cells (soma) and that the soma or non-sex cells have no effect on hereditary information. The metaphysical ramifications of Weissmann's theory is that the essence of the life form, what is not lost, is only given in terms of reproduction, that the creative power of an organism is only ever sexed. The Freudian consequences of this will be discussed in the conclusion.

Following from his resistance to Weissmann, Pearson then sums up the thrust of his text as attempting to circumvent the "two nihilisms of modernity, the potential nihilism of Weismann's germ-plasmic finality and the perceived nihilism of Freud's death-drive."[46] The latter nihilism will be addressed at this text's conclusion and in regards to the former we can only say that Weismann does not go far enough. Given the fact that Weissmann's germ-plasm suggests some infinitude to life we must answer with "more nihilism!"

Whereas Weissmann's germ-plasm asserts the discardability of individual bodies for the force of life, Pearson suggests that Deleuze is concerned with an ethics that works from clearly meaningful bodies and hopes to maximize the affective passions between them, to create an odd dynamism of joy.[47] That is, for Deleuze and for Pearson, it is not enough that life lives only to die and perpetually (till the decoherence of all matter in the universe) refuel other forms of life. In this sense life is given a much more reserved openness than the openness of Negarestani and Thacker mentioned above since life needs a push more than adaptation and survival and is lamented in an ethics of affective passion, in life needing to feel good.[48] Life is not a complex transmission of joy, it is a flow of biomass subject to forces far beyond its sensibility.

The lesson of Weissmann then is that there is something about life which goes beyond individual forms of life. As Merelau-Ponty points out in his text *Nature*, Jacob von Uexküll's protoplasms participate in such horror, in the indifference of life, in that the amoeba is a pure productivity moved by and caught in the pure productivity of nature, something that flows with the dynamics of nature itself.[49]

The difference between life (as a force, as a propensity towards the formation of organisms) and individual forms of life indexes the larger problems of life and being which, as Thacker suggests are related by negation.[50] In other words the problem is what is non-being in relation to life, is there something in life that is living but is not yet classifiable?[51] As Thacker sums up nicely, Life has been used conceptually yet the conception of life has no discernible definition.[52]

The gap between the viral world and the fungus world, as we will see, is one of seemingly mechanized organization – that is the slime and ooze from which we came is not so unsettling since it appears (for us) as that dead matter which is waiting for potentiation whereas the slime mold, the fungus, appears as the same kind of matter but that which is active of its own accord. In other words, for the viral thought seems able to organize and subdue the life-meaning of the virus whereas, as we shall see in the next chapter, the fungal begins to escape and contorts the bounds of our way of thinking life in an external fashion...

There is, of course, little if no difference between the activity of life in the viral and in the fungoid in an ontological sense. There is no special form of life in one or the other as nature is, all along, interpenetrating everything around us and our slimy selves as well.

I.2

Fungoid Horror and The Creep of Life

"[...]the fungi, which occupy so considerable a place in the
vegetable world, feed like animals: whether they are ferments,
saprophytes or parasites, it is to already formed organic
substances that they owe their nourishment. [...] It is a
remarkable fact that the fungi, which nature has spread all over
the earth in such extraordinary profusion, have not been able to
evolve [...] They might be called the abortive children of the
vegetable world."
Henri Bergson, Creative Evolution,

"The function of mushrooms is to rid the world of old rubbish."
John Cage

Where in the previous chapter the uneasy relationship of productivity and decay was largely human centered and interior here we are addressing the spread of the sliminess of life in an exterior and more ecological sense. Historically, fungus played an important geophysical role as an early formation of slime corroded the dull rocky surface of the earth leading to the creation of soil. In popular culture fungus shows up as sprouting patches of mushrooms from the black earth alongside the bleakness of gravestones, catacombs, and within cracked arcane tunnels. Fungus is ancient and always in the orbit of death, decay, and dampness.

Take the following passage from weird fiction writer Thomas Ligotti's short tale "The Shadow at the Bottom of the World":

In sleep we were consumed by the feverish life of the earth, cast among a ripe, fairly rotting world of strange growths and transformation. We took a place within a darkly flourishing landscape where even the air was ripened into ruddy hues and everything wore the wrinkled grimace of decay, the mottled complexion of old flesh. The face of the land itself was knotted with so many other faces, ones that were corrupted by vile impulses. Grotesque expressions were molding themselves into the darkish grooves of ancient bark and the whorls of withered leaf; pulpy, misshapen features peered out of damp furrows; and the crisp skin of stalks and dead seeds split into a multitude of crooked smiles. All was a freakish mask painted with russet, rashy colors—colors that bled with a virulent intensity, so rich and vibrant that things trembled with their own ripeness.[53]

In their *Romance of the Fungus World,* RT Rolfe and FW Rolfe point to an odd attitude towards fungi in scientific, literary and other communities, highlighting a sweeping condemnation of fungi as part of a widespread fungiphobia.[54] Rolfe and Rolfe justify this phobia through a brief survey of fungi in folklore and fiction, which shows a persistent association with pestilence, death and as "agents of dissolution."[55] Fungi clear the forest floor of organic debris and subsequently vitalize the nutrients of the dead thereby making space for new life. Fungi disintegrate their organic neighbors through secretions[56] as well as rhizomatic expansion.[57]

Beyond the organic, fungus dissolves inorganic structures and is vilified for its damage to manmade ones in particular. As Rolfe and Rolfe show, stories such as Poe's "Fall of the House of Usher" are replete with descriptions of rot and fungi.[58] This de-structuring of fungus can be spread to the faltering spatial dimension of ancient history in general, of the deterioration of old texts, of faded ruins, to the stretch of all civilized space which crumbles indefinitely in time. Jeff Vandermeer's steampunk novel *Shriek* and its precursor *City of Saints and Madmen* embrace this theme clearly. The setting of both novels, the city of Ambergris, is a place where the original inhabitants, a race of sentient mushrooms called the gray caps, were forced underground. Vandermeer's book is an oddity of form constituted by a thrice edited manuscript which suggests the unreliability of all its narrators as well as history itself (history being the main concern of the text both familial and on a wider scale). Vandermeer's texts infuse genealogical history with the hallucinatory and unpredictability of fungus forming a decaying yet growing patchwork form of history, a history that, in its very form, is rotting to mush.[59]

The fungoid, the fundamental creepiness of life, displays the unhinged spatiality of life as well as its rampant ungrounding, of the very surface which seems necessary in order to sustain it and all other life forms. Evident in the above epigraph, Thomas Ligotti's tales are replete with fungus as a simultaneous operative of gross life and perpetual decay. In the "Bungalow House" the narrator becomes obsessed with an odd local artist who describes an old bungalow house, with a "threadbare carpet" of "verminous bodies," and filled with "naturally revolting forms."[60]

Furthermore, in Ligotti's "Severini" the narrator discusses the odd artist Severini and the works of his followers which are classified under the unofficial name "the nightmare of the organism"[61] The most relevant title of these fictional works being "The Descent into the Fungal."[62]

Severini himself lives in a small shack out in the jungle, described as a "tropical sewer"[63] sitting amidst trees and vines where there were "giant flowers that smelled like rotting meat" in the fungus and muck.[64] The followers of Severini dream of a temple amidst a fetid landscape with "the walls seeping with slime and soft with mold."[65]

The sight of Severini's shack is unbearable to the narrator as he states that "I never looked directly into the pools of oozing life" and that, unlike the others, he did not "wish to exist as a fungus exists or as a form of multi-colored slime mold exists."[66] Ligotti's narrator promptly burns the place to the ground. The characters of "Severini" dangerously short-circuit the generative slime of unbound growth and the slime as the morass of the decayed linked together as "that great black life from which we have all emerged and of which we are all made."[67]

To swing back to literal fungus, the intertwining of life and death has long been a mark of fungoid existence, with the death and darknesses of forests being populated by fungus which thrives in the hollow remnants of more majestic vegetative growth. In this sense, fungus is representative of death and not another form of life. The fungal marks the unnerving transitive nature of somaticism – the food of the dead and the fruiting bodies. Fungal bodies are thus hardly bodies at all as they stretch the conceptual limits of their own bodies as well as destroy and decay the purportedly solidity of other bodies. Yet such processes are hardly restrictive to the mushroom. The first of the four stages of decomposition (fresh, bloat, decay and dry) is autolysis – when the cells of a living thing self destruct as the body essentially begins to consume itself. The fungal merely aid the process of decomposition, of decay, by thriving in layers of generative putrefaction. Whereas decay is the breakdown of tissues following the cessation of an organism's life, putrefaction is the aided process of life breaking down. If there is a central disgust to fungus, or to plant life in general, it is because creeping life is a life stripped down to its mechanisms, processes, and breakdowns.

To return to fictional territory, Stanley Weinbaum's proto-plasmic monsters of an impossible Venus, located in tropical jungles in his stories "Parasite Planet" and "The Lotus Eaters" expand on the inherently disgusting nature of plant life and particularly of fungus. The atmosphere of Weinbaum's Venus is filled with "uncounted millions of the spores of those fierce Venusian molds" capable of sprouting "in furry and nauseating masses."[68] The Venusian jungles contain a terrible scene as "avid and greedy life was emerging, wriggling mud grass and the bulbous fungi called "walking balls. And all around a million little slimy creatures slithered across the mud, eating each other rapaciously, being torn to bits, and each fragment re-forming to a complete creature."[69] The oddest of Weinbaum's creatures is the doughpot which Weinbaum descibes as "a nauseous creature. It's a mass of white, dough-like protoplasm, ranging in size from a single cell to perhaps twenty tons of mushy filth. It has no fixed form; in fact, it's merely a mass of de Proust cells—in effect, a disembodied, crawling, hungry cancer."[70] In the sequel Weinbaum's protagonist encounters the lotus eaters, strange veined and bulbous creatures which state that they do not need or desire to survive but only must reproduce with spores – growing tumor-like on one another. One of the lotus eaters says life has no meaning, life is not something to fight for.[71]

Weinbaum's alien fungi are part of a larger tradition of fictional strangeness of fungal forms. Again following Rolfe and Rolfe, this strangeness is found in HG Wells' *The First Men in the Moon*[72] and Jules Verne's *The Journey to the Center of the Earth*.[73] In this vein, but also by pointing towards actually fungi, Weinbaum's extraterrestial extension of the sporaceous function of the fungal uncomfortably warps the internal in order to pollute the external.

Spores allow fungal life, as an amorphous creep, to extend itself into the vertical and to survive unfavorable conditions as thick walled spheres or as more parasitic entities which germinate inside host creatures or spread from the infected host to further spread again either as an interiority or extended exter-nality. Whereas flowering plants are considered higher life forms working in conjunction with nature, cryptogams (fungus) appear to feed on nature itself and are considered a lower or simpler form of organism.[74]

As Negarestani puts it "The spore, or endo-bacterial dust, is a relic with untraceable zones of migration and traversal, a swarm-particle creeping off the radar screen; a speck of dust you never know whether you have inhaled or not."[75] We could also mention Bergson's invocation of life as being composed of eddies of dust.[76] On the theme of inhalation and the senses, some fungi use a malodorous stench to attract insects. These fungi, in the family Phallaceae, can smell like dung or carrion to attract vectors of fungal spread (such as flies), again tying the specter of death to the germinal spread of life as well as binding the miasmic life-of-death to the demonic evidenced in the names of some fungus such as Devil's Snuff Box and Devil's Stink-pot.[77] Furthermore, of the minority of fungus which attack warm blooded animals, the majority infiltrate through the inhalations of the lungs adding a realistic sense of wariness to the rotten smell of the fungus.

The aforementioned dark (bio) vitalism of Ligotti's creeping nature is anticipated by some of the fungoid creatures of Lovecraft's pantheon as well as William Hope Hodgson's short tales "The Derelict" and especially his well known "The Voice in the Night."

Hodgson's "The Voice in the Night" tells the story of a shipwrecked crew that becomes infected and slowly transmogrified by a gray fungus leaving them nodding lumps. Beyond the creeping horror of the fungus – it also fills the victims with an "inhuman desire" to consume the sweet tasting matter, to consume the long dead corpses of others that have been slowly grown over. Hodgson describes the miserable island of fungus thusly: "In places it rose into horrible, fantastic mounds, which seemed almost to quiver, as with a quiet life, when the wind blew across them. Here and there it took on the forms of vast fingers, and in others it just spread out flat and smooth and treacherous. Odd places, it appeared as grotesque stunted trees, seeming extraordinarily kinked and gnarled – the whole quaking vilely at times."[78]

In "The Derelict" the encounter is far more rapid and terrifying. A ship of men aboard an abandoned vessel find themselves barely able to escape with their lives as a brown squelching fungus attempts to consume them. The active/passive divide of the fungoid horror is replicated in fictional fields as a form of trap and an assailant, a trap in its psychedelic spore launching form and an assailant in its aggressively consumptive modality.

This putrid fungal pantheon is formalized and maintained in the literature of several role playing games such as the *Dungeons and Dragons* monster manual. Creatures with the names Phantom Fungus, Shambling Mound, Shrieker, Yellow Musk Creeper and so forth fill the book, creating a taxonomy of fungal horrors that speak to the seemingly endless morphology of fungal creep and toxicological capacity. This fungoid monsters furthermore introduce the uncomfortable notion of plant movement, of the base creepiness of the creep.

The question becomes what is the limit of the creeping mechanism, of the stretch of the creep?

In the previous chapter we saw the explosive internality of life whereas the fungal appears to be an infinite expansion of the already extended, an endless development of the odd spatiality of the fungoid, of the sick perpetuation of foul matter being simultaneously the cause as well as the result. The fungal operates as a counter to the apparent somatism of vegetative life due to the space-traversing capacity of molds, mushrooms and other crawling bits of dark vegetative forms. Whereas life in evolution can be construed as merely mutations on variations on a form, fungus appears as only vegetative variations without form. One could also consider Rolf Sattler's take on plant morphology in which leaves are not a plant structure with processes but the leaves are processes themselves. Following Sattler, fungi would then be pure materialized process, or materiality as simply the production of production where the distinction between body and intensity or more basically matter and energy is abnegated.

Fungus then seems, at least how we have viewed it thus far, to embody extended mutation to the degree that it moves and grows in the sphere of nature itself, functioning as a kind of living landscape. One aspect of the insectoid Zerg species in the videogame *Starcraft* series is a nightmarish play on this theme; the Zerg must grow an organic carpet in order for their infra-structure and war machine (or war organism) to develop and spread. The bio-matter plane is called the creep by the non-Zerg – a biological plasma threatening to fill/cover the totality of space itself. The creep grows over, but does not extend through, 'empty' space itself - it fills the full, it remains grounded yet the sporous allows new terrestrial unconnected zones to be plagued by the fungus.

Returning to Hodgson's fungus, we see, on the other hand, that he extends biology beyond such absolute space and intro-duces the truly horrifying aspect of biology as endlessly spatial and naturally mutated, as growth unbound. The disturbing possibility that Lovecraft cultivates for instance, is that there are monstrosities that will live far beyond us; the possibility of a something that "whirled blindly past ghastly midnights of rotting creation, corpses of dead worlds with sores that were cities"[79] would continue to torment us. Put another way, Lovecraft extends biology to terrifyingly vast temporal as well as spatial limits. Where the mucous-like creep of the Zerg assumes a knowable limit to space time, Lovecraft questions even this boundary.

In his tale "The Dream-Quest of Unknown Kadatth" Lovecraft describes Azathoth (an Outer god like Nyarlathotep) as "that shocking final peril which gibbers unmentionably outside the ordered universe," that "last amorphous blight of nethermost confusion which blashphemes and bubbles at the

33

centre of all infinity" who "gnaws hungrily in inconceivable, unlighted chambers beyond time."[80] Azathoth's name may have multiple origins but the most striking is the alchemy term azoth which is both a cohesive agent and a acidic creation pointing back to the generative and decayed status of slime in Ligotti's work as well as Weinbaum's disgusting Venusian doughpot.

To return closer to the topic at hand, Lovecraft engages in his own descent into the fungal especially in his "Fungus from Yuggoth" a set of sonnets depicting his reality of cosmic horror where the twenty first piece is titled Nyarlathotep and the twenty second Azathoth. In his sonnets Lovecraft seems to move between Ligotti's horror-of-origins and Hodgson's monstrousness, but staying with mostly formless creations. Lovecraft's utilization of the fungal can be seen as attempting an assault on the senses in various modes, appealing to the most base disgust of life, of being an organism (as Ligotti does) as well as portraying the awful pliability of the fungal and the vegetative, as the inevitable creep of life, not as life as always enduring but as always dying, as always being ready to be consumed. Michel Houellebecq, whose engagement with Lovecraft will we examine more closely later, points this out in his *H.P. Lovecraft: Against the World, Against Life* when he points out the inherently disgusting quality of Lovecraft's reality.[81]

From the fourth sonnet of Lovecraft's Fungi:
"The day had come again, when as a child
I saw - just once - that hollow of old oaks,
Grey with a ground-mist that enfolds and chokes
The slinking shapes which madness has defiled.
It was the same - an herbage rank and wild"[82]

And from the fourteenth:

"What fungi sprout in Yuggoth, and what scents

And tints of flowers fill Nithon's continents,
Such as in no poor earthly garden blow.
Yet for each dream these winds to us convey,
A dozen more of ours they sweep away!"[83]

Lovecraft plays on these themes in the aforementioned "Dream-Quest..." in the following way: "In the tunnels of that twisted wood, whose low prodigious oaks twine groping boughs and shine dim with the phosphoresence of strange fungi."[84] The rank smell of fungus leads to its unnatural iridescence, partially lighting the way for a descent into the horrible.

Taking a another step into the swamp, Lovecraft's compatriot Clark Ashton Smith's Tsathoggua Cycle and Lovecraft's own "Whisper in Darkness" discusses the filth-god Tsathoggua. Tsathoggua is an amorphous toad-like creature and his servitors are black formless spawn which reside in a rotting basin of slime. The smell of rot obscured or contained within creation, reasserts our aversion to new life when it is shed of its humanistic shell, Tsathoggua attempts to return us to the cesspool of evolution without the blanket of telology or designed betterment. From Clark Ashton Smith's "The Tale of Satampra Zeiros": "though unsurpassably foul, was nevertheless not an odor of putrefaction, but resembled rather the smell of some vile and unclean creature of the marshes. The odor was almost beyond endurance, and we were about to turn away when we perceived a slight ebullition of the surface, as if the sooty liquid were being agitated from within by some submerged animal or other entity. This ebullition increased rapidly, the center swelled as if with the action of some powerful yeast, and we watched in utter horror, while an uncouth amorphous head with dull and bulging eyes arose gradually on an ever-lengthening neck, and stared us in the face with primordial malignity."[85]

Again, to return to the briefly mentioned theory of miasma, where the causes of disease are the result of bad air which is often thought as merely an outmoded theory of disease production, here we are concerned with the production-from/of-rot of which miasma is the strongest representative. The tropical sewer of Ligotti mentioned above is fundamentally miasmic as well, where particular stenches are indicative of the production of death and decay, of the exumate materials resulting from organic forms moving towards creating new organisms in the biosphere.

The production of life requires decay and a clearing a way of the biosphere space to make room for new species. As we have seen, the spore production of fruiting bodies, of the sexual polyp of a particular fungus, mirrors the bad air aspect of spreading an infective form of life. The stench of death is also the stench of fertilization, of a turning over in the churning teeth of nature. This biological and geological churning is Vandermeer's crumbling history and the horridness of all creation, and the interplexing relation of degradation and generation.

One of Houellebecq's poems tie the two together:

"Deep in some woods, on a carpet of moss,
Foetid tree trunks survive their leaves;
Around them develops an atmosphere of mourning;
Their skin filthy and black, mushrooms pushing through it"[86]

Houellebecq's poem echoes the darker passages of Percy Shelley's "The Sensitive Plant," in its depiction of the morbid fecundity of vegetative nature.[87] The possibility of plant death, of the rottenness of poetic and beautiful nature is followed by the emergence of sickly fungus.

As Negarestani points out however, decay is not merely a clean integration of life and death but the summoning of irresolution, of an unsettling and infinite softening.[88] The fungal, as the spatial extension of unified production and decay is ultimately troublesome as it appears as a corrupting production.

This corrupting production raises an interesting link between the organic of the fungus and the inorganic on which it grows and spreads. The softening of the terrestrial where the fungus regrounds (cracks, and breaks apart the hardest materials) but doesn't unground the terrestrial completely.

The fungal becomes the deathly embodiment of the terrestrial-generative, "it was though the sick earth had burst into foul pustules"[89] or, in one strange outmoded theory, fungus was the corrupted earth itself caused by the energy delivered by lightning.[90]

The softening of the fungal and the de- and un- earthing of the vegetative becomes troubling when it encounters the living body of humans or other physical creatures intersect the fungal. While we have already discussed the degradation of the organic by the fungal, what is extra troubling is the fact that the fungal threatens to undo the necessity of the body, of the form for life. It was already mentioned that the fungal stretches the bodily limit of life as well as takes apart the solidity of other forms of life and, as we have seen, crumbles the purportedly one sided relation between inorganic nature (such as the planet) and organic life. Once this distinction falls apart the very liveliness of life is no longer traceable to the organic or to any identifiable form of life, but is immediately debased. Before reaching this point however solidity requires further dissolution.

The ultimate example of such horrifying undermining of solidity paired with somatic is the muck monster – the creatures taken from the tradition of the Judaic golem but exorcised of religiosity – such as the heap, man-thing, swamp thing to the great sludge enemy of Godzilla - Hedorah and so forth. Muck monsters which range from the dumb automaton (the Golem) to the comic book hero, put thought too close to nature, decorporealizing that which is supposed to be properly formed in order to think. As we have seen the decorporealizing processes of the fungal are met by a recycling and rebuilding (through spatial expansion) thereby undermining the humanistic solidity of its fixed boundaries complicating the difference between sense and thought, between life as bound and life as creeping. Philosophically speaking, muck monsters provide a degradation of phenomenology in that thought becomes another object in the pile of nature and not the sole means of determining nature through the senses. This residue or base connectivity of life can be seen in Negarstani's brief comment on the Menstruum or living mud. The Menstruum works as a "communicational entity" between elements and can be taken as a kind of stuff of life.[91]

Again, returning to Lovecraft, his Shoggoth which appears as "a shapeless congeries of protoplasmic bubbles, faintly self-luminous, and with myriads of temporary eyes forming and un-forming as pustules of greenish light all over the tunnel-filling front that bore down upon us"[92] questions the purportedly necessity of a shape to life and to intelligence, to the necessity of a identifiable entity as being something we need to recognize, the suggestion that if something thinks, and even more, if something reasons and is a form of life it must not be a complete assault on the senses.

The amorphousness of fungal life indexes life's reliance not on the necessary thinkability of life but, as evidence above, its connection to the earth, to the inorganic, and the long strand of succession of physical and chemical forms leading to its accidental development. The spatiality of fungal life as different from the networked life of contagion (of time overcoming space) is the spatial over coming of time, the revenge of an old earth and old life being reinscribed and mutated against itself as in the case of Iain Hamilton Grant's anti-somatic Schelling.

Again life becomes that of being trapped between (bare) matter and mattering (being generative and mattering, and having meaning). We will address the possible rampancy of the organic in the following chapter, questioning the possibility of life across multiple biospheres and its relation to nature on the cosmic scale.

I.3

Extra-Galactic Terror

"They knew that every system, whether mechanical or biological, eventually runs down [...] The tyranids had found the only possible remedy for this. They moved from galaxy to galaxy, harvesting fresh, newly evolved DNA with which to renew and reinvigorate their own. They were the universes' ultimate life form. Quite possibly they had existed forever, and would continue to exist forever."[93]

"The cosmos...is simply a perpetual rearrangement of electrons which is constantly seething as it always has been and always will be. Our tiny globe and puny thoughts are but one momentary incident in its eternal mutation."[94]

Life as we have formulated it so far is subdued by the forces of time and space and yet the intensive interiority of the viral seems to challenge these bounds as does the externality of the fungal. The question that remains is what is life, what is the force of life, and what are the forces that act on life. The task is to answer these questions without venturing too much towards the immaterial or unscientific. The issue becomes the thinkability of life, thinking life, and the life of thought. Or, put in other words how do we define life, what is it about life that allows it to think, and what is the future of thought's rootedness in life. We will pursue these issues through fictional superorganic entities.

The superorganic is conceptually constructed by combining the devastating emergence of the miniscule (such as the virus) coupled with the spatial expansion found in the fungoid – it is, in other terms, the exacerbated capacity of the swarm on a colossal scale. As was discussed in the introduction the swarm is the form of life that presents itself as most problematic for thinking; both by producing the results of thought without intelligence (we observe non-thinking entities acting as if they can think) and as being hard to think-as-life (we are not sure if the swarm itself is a thing), as we saw in the introduction, because of the indeterminacy between the part and the whole of life.

The hybridization of the viroid and fungoid (creating a life that transmogrifies and creeps) can be tied to the theory of exogenesis. The theory of exogenesis holds that life has always already existed and that life on earth has come from elsewhere. At some point in the distance past a gaia spore, or object carrying early forms of, or the necessary ingredients for creating life, would have reached the early earth seeding it.

Concepts of panspermia have been suggested for hundreds of years: the theoretical biologist Frederick Kielmeyer suggested such a concept in the 1800s.[95] While romantic notions of cosmic ancestry can be taken from such a concept the more troubling suggestion is the possible age of certain forms of life and the rampancy of any particular form of extremophile, of a creature which can exist in seemingly impossible conditions. The fungal spores of last chapter and the viroids of the first being examples of such lifeforms.

As we have seen however, empirical and speculative biology provides ample evidence in favor of such a conceptualization of rampant life. Anxiety about the bounds of a biological life and the fragility of any one form of species-being is unearthed by the extinct traces of animals and exacerbated by the science fictive particularly in terms of an array of insectoid superorganisms; a tradition begun by the endoparasitoidic (parasitic to the point of death) xenomorph of the *Aliens* series.

The xenomorph has a distinctly Lovecraftian genealogy as the creature's design came from a work by the surrealist artist HR Giger titled Necromicon, named after the central fictional text of strange demonological lore by the invented mad Arab Abdul Alhazred which describes the Cthulu mythos, the grimoire of strange ancient monstrousities which populate the universe as well as dimensions outside of it, entities such as the Great Old Ones. The xenomorphs imitate hive-minded insects as they mindlessly follow the orders of their queen and act only to propagate their vile species. The Lovecraftian influence comes from the weird and amorphousness of alien life which he created; aliens with almost imperceptible forms and near god-like powers. The result of Lovecraft's mythos is the minimization of the human race, a depressive expansion of the Great Chain of Being where instead of an omnipotent god at one end with humans not far beneath, there is only an ever stretching stream of entities with humanity lost in its perilous contortion. Or, as Gould points out via Freud, each scientific advance means the further existential dethronement of homosapiens in the universe.[96]

This lostness and dethronement is redoubled temporally following the natural history of Carl Friedrich Kielmeyer who through his focus on extinction events revealed a nature in which humanity's place is not only tenuous due to other possible organisms but due to the small span of time we have occupied.[97] For Kielmeyer a species' ability to reproduce, to fill time, is what might guarantee its future survival.[98]

As Michel Houellebecq writes in *HP Lovecraft: Against the World, Against Life*: "It is possible, in fact, that beyond the narrow range of our perception, other entities exist. Other creatures, other races, other concepts and other minds. Amongst these entities some are probably far superior to us in intelligence and in knowledge. But this is not necessarily good news."[99]

Lovecraft contorts the very concept of a taxonomy to its temporal and spatial limits submitting to us that organic life itself barely gets in the way of the cosmic course of time (and space) when he writes "we imagine that the welfare of our race is the paramount consideration, when as a matter of fact the very existence of the race may be an obstacle to the predestined course of the aggregated universes of infinity!"[100]

Under Lovecraft's indifferentism humans become just another form of matter in the universe, simply another form of entropic fodder in a mechanistic cosmos. Lovecraft's indifference is deeply connected, as ST Joshi has shown, to his commitment to the work of Ernst Haeckel.[101] Haeckel was a zoologist in Germany at the turn of the 20th century known widely for his recapitulation theory which states that an organism in development went through the developments of the particular species on the whole. Haeckel, in at least partial agreement with Weissmann, states that individual life is generally sacrificial, as only a small fragment of life at large. Lovecraft's materialism, again following Joshi, becomes after some time, far more obscured than Haeckel's.[102] Yet Haeckel's germ plasm maintains a Lovecraftian flavor in that life in general is a force that cannot be reduced to particular organisms with organisms only being an excrescence, a bud a sprout.[103]

The important point of Lovecraft's bestiary is not he designated his creatures as not supernatural, but as supernormal, keeping nature in in all its monstrous capacity.[104] Lovecraft speaks of the tension between the natural and the unnatural is his short story "The Unnameable." He writes: "[...] if the psychic emanations of human creatures be grotesque distortions, what coherent representation could express or portray so gibbous and infamous a nebulousity as the spectre of a malign, chaotic perversion, itself a morbid blasphemy against Nature?"[105] Lovecraft explores exactly the tension outlined at the beginning of this chapter, between life and thought. At the end of his short tale Lovecraft compounds the problem as the unnameable is described as "a gelatin—a slime—yet it had shapes, a thousand shapes of horror beyond all memory."[106]

Another realm where thought insufficiently grasps the rampancy of biological life is the often unimaginative work of xenobiologists. As Jack Cohen and Ian Stewart discuss in "Alien

Science" much of contemporary xenobiology is so narrow as to exclude organisms that exist on the earth, creatures capable of thriving in extreme environments such as near heat vents or fungus inside the light-less interior of the Chernobyl sarcophagus. That is, the criteria for alien life would pass over many species already identified here on earth.

It would be safe to say that the speculated xenobiological capacities of life are underestimated whereas in the science fictive, the organic is exacerbated to the extreme. From the Tyranids of *Warhammer 40,000* to the Zerg of *Starcraft*, to Species 8472 of *Star Trek* to the Yuuzhan Vong of *Star Wars*, the rampant organic becomes the most threatening form of life, as a pure life or life as mutagen which is always inadmissible to the intergallactic bodies of government. Furthermore the transformation of the organic as hidden internality (in the germinal or the viroid) moving towards externality as only a kind of unfolding (in the Deleuzo-Guattarian sense) is externalized as a form of techne, as an exterior painting of the swarming absolute. Put another way, the biological is seen as only a base that, when overly expansive, is grotesque where civilization is the appropriate externalizaton of a life form's creative capabilities.

In other words, any continuous evolution of an alien species requires a technological separation between uncivilized organicism and cultured technologized life.

In other words the minute ungroundings of the microorganic (growth and decay) meet the planetary ungroundings of the monstrous (whether organic or inorganic) in the science fictive.

Of all the aforementioned fictional species the richest is the Tyranids.

"The Tyranids are an alien race from the colds depths of the void that hunger constantly for warm flesh. They infest the stars in their billions, a raw force of destruction that has been likened to a locust swarm."[107] Whereas Lovecraft's Cthulloid Old Ones programatically tampered with the dwindling destiny of the human race by manufacturing certain "protoplasmic masses" on earth,[108] the Tyranids are not so patient; treating the human race as merely another form of biological matter to be absorbed. This gelatinous origin is invoked by Bergson's *Creative Evolution* where he states that if there is a connectivity to all life it is in this original slimy moment.

In the backstory for the nightmarish race which appears as a massive body of claws and talons, once a world's defenses have been sufficiently beaten back and deadly spores have been spread across the planet, the Tyranids consume all the biomass on the planetoid rendering it in pools of acid. This gruel forms the fuel and material for future Tyranid mutates, so they can continue their onslaught across the inhabited systems of the universe. The Tyranid's unstoppable march across inhabited space questions the limit of the concept of eco-system and of eco-space in particular. Can all the inhabited universes make up one bit of eco-space, can one species fill it all?

By the civilized races of the universe the Tyranids are considered a monstrosity, as something fundamentally opposed to progressivity.[109] That is, the Tyranids despite their sentience (at least on a hive level if not on an individual level) are considered as a non-civilization given their rabid mutative nature. Tyranid technology is of course non-separable from their biological contours it seems technological only in that it seems it should be separated.[110] As Henri Bergson notes, one of the fundamental issues separating humans from other animals is the separation of technology from the body, from instinctual behaviors.[111]

To connect back to our viral chapter, alien invasion films such as *War of the Worlds* and *Independence Day*, the viral and/or bacterial is the only thing that is capable of circumventing alien technologies whereas the Tyranids are an extension of the viral itself. But, since the viral nature of the Tyranids is extended to the height of intergalactic war, their gross mindlessness is somehow worse than unjust or perverse motivations for war because even malicious reason is still reason, because the operation of thought is ontologically raised above the biological.

Why is the species-being of the Tyranid nightmarish whereas the war mongering nature of humans and other species is absolved of a certain horribleness given the avenues of religion, politics, nationality and so forth. The horrible extended internalness of the Tyranid, that is, the revolting extension of the biological to the level of what is commonly thought of as removed from us (technology, war machines et cetera) becomes only a natural extension. The primordial sliminess of being is thus returned through via the over extension of the biological in the speculative monsters of the Tyranids. This sliminess is accentuated in the lack of free will amongst the Tyranids, as free will is thought as an outgrowth of nature that escapes its bounds, a part of nature that is, at its center unnatural.

The following passage sums these themes up nicely: "Tyranids travel the galaxies and the voids between them in vast, drifting hive fleets. These consist of millions of sentient craft, each in turn home to untold numbers of monstrosities evolved from the bubbling geno-organs of their mucous-slicked reproductive chambers."[112]

At some point biology is expected to give in to the force of reason as itself exterior to it, in a seemingly impossible way. As Grant says following Oken: "The culmination of Biology is the destruction of individuals, which is held in check so long as there remains something."[113] Given human ego-centrism this something is often viewed as intelligence. The question becomes that of intelligence and in particular reason as taking over the biological but the concept of the swarm (again, of emergence) causes problems for any deliberate cleavage.

Cohen and Stewart argue that intelligence is a universal yet such universality has no metaphysical implications.[114] The issue is not to assert that intelligence must happen but that intelligence, what Cohen and Stewart define as the ability to manip-ulate world models tends to happen.[115] Extilligence, the ability to externalize our intelligence, to record what has been done so humans need not reinvent all of what they have with the death of every generation.[116] Yet how does one separate the exteriority of intelligence from extilligence, that is, is it a clear matter of separating what seems what must be a result of thought and the thinking in terms of the organic?

Given the capacities of intelligence, is it possible to avoid the valorization of intelligence, the celebration of intelligence over nature, since we need intelligence to think it, or can nature be saved as the productive engine of all intelligence? No one expounded the possibility of the former view more strongly than Fichte and no one pursued the latter more admirably then as the naturephilosopher F.W.J. von Schelling.

Schelling made motions towards unbinding thought though me must remain cautious of his potentially romantic inclinations. Schelling argued that nature reflected the work of intelligence (since it had to eventually in a merely practical way), allow for the eventual emergence of thinking. As soon as humans are separated from nature Schelling warned, nature becomes a dead object.[117]

In Schelling's *Ideas for a Philosophy of Nature* Schelling posits the Absolute as the unity of thinking and nature.[118] The unity of the real and the ideal is both real and ideal in an identitarian way, that is in terms of a thought simultaneity but not a temporal or historical simultaneity. That is, the withdrawnness of nature restricts the ideal but the ideal also moves forward in time.[119]

Put more directly, while nature precedes thinking, we can think nature as unified both in a real sense (thought is produced by brains which are the results of long and slow evolutionary processes and is part of nature) but thought is both ideally unified with nature because thought can produce like nature produces – in a seemingly uninhibited fashion.

Schelling is often relegated as a mere philosophical stepping stone between the idealism of Fichte and the Dialectic of Hegel. Fichte asserted the entire complex of nature as the not-I as that which merely opposes itself to the capabilities of the I, of the self.[120] Hegel can be seen as taking this idealism to its logical limit, not opposed the I and not I but by setting up nature as a kind of exhausted spirit, spirit being being what propels the self, the I. In both accounts nature is given little appreciation reduced to either an obstacle or as a by-product of the work of the self. Schelling, on the other hand particularly in his early works, is adamant about the necessary material pre-condition of all thought and all being. Nature is completely indifferent to human existence how is it then that intelligence is removed from the developments of nature?[121]

How does the concept of valorized intelligence manifest itself?

Warren Fahy's *Fragment* provides an interesting account of the perceived division (in terms of value) between intelligence and the biological. In the novel an isolated island is discovered where evolution has taken a very different path, producing highly unusual creatures such as disc-shaped ants, eight legged spider cats and carnivorous plants. A group of scientists speculate as to have the bizarre species came to be with one invoking a radicalized view of Haeckle.[122]

The human villain of the story, Thatcher Redmond proposes that the hyper-violent biosphere of the island is perfect because it is absent of an intelligent species,[123] his theory being that humans are the biggest threat to the earth because of their intelligence.[124] He states that "Intelligent life is an environmental cancer."[125]

Redmond's theory falls apart when the expedition team discovers (and is saved by) an intelligent life form which the scientists decide they must save from the looming nuclear bombardment simply because the creature's intelligence makes it more human.[126] The narratological shift in attitude based on the discovery of the intelligent ape in the novel betrays its initial Lovecraftian aspects, immediately becoming a humanist celebration of life and of the capacity of intelligence to stabilize life[127] lending itself to an uncritical ecological positivity.

Fahy's dismissal of the capacities of radical biology in the face of intelligence in popular fiction confirms Schelling's misgivings surrounding the dominant treatment of nature in philosophy. This treatment denies that nature is prior to thinking,[128] that the ideal must be explained through the real[129] and that man sublates nature, placing ourselves at the peak of its production.[130]

Schelling's genetic philosophy of nature is situated in the romantic era of science creating a tension between the scientific investigation of life and the aesthetic concerns of German Idealism. Schelling's articulation of thought however is not blindly romantic in that it ignores, or at least problematizes, anthrocentricism, it is unromantic precisely in its assertion that humanity cannot escape the base material nature of existence.

As Robert Richards points out in *The Romantic Conception of Life*, Schelling placed organisms at the center of his philosophy of nature and set up the absolute, the central entity of his philosophy, as an organically functioning entity.[131] Schelling developed his notion of the organic (and of the absolute as organic) from his contemporaries in the natural sciences namely Humboldt, Blumenbach, Keilmeyer, and Reil.[132]

However, as Iain Hamilton Grant points out in his *Philosophies of Nature after Schelling*, Schelling's philosophy cannot be reduced to only the organism and has its roots in a multitude of issues and, in particular the issue of temporality.[133] As Grant writes: "The philosophy of natural history from the seventeenth to the nineteenth centuries was structured around the problems of reality as against the phenomenality of time."[134]

For Schelling, nature is both product and productivity, the

products being formed by two forces opposing one another, the negative force retarding the positive it in the form of a whirlpool[135] which can also be thought of as an infinite development of ideal archetypes in nature which are attempted in time and space but are never perfectible.[136] In many ways Schelling's philosophy prefigures powers metaphysics in that there are productive and restrictive powers in nature as well as archetypes or patterns.

The product and production relation of Schelling's nature should not be seen as supporting the somaticism or body-composition of nature which, as we saw in the last chapter, bio-weapon inspired thought begins to rally against.[137] The question which Grant raises in relation to the biology of Kielmeyer is whether the use of a slime, and protoplasm in particular, always asserts a somaticism, always asserts that microbodies are additive or that macrobodies (such as viewing the earth as one organism) are divisible in nature.[138] For Kielmeyer, while bodies or points within nature are pivotal, it is not bodies that are the source and measure of nature but a net of forces which operate on those bodies and ultimately on thought.[139]

As mentioned in the introduction, Schelling attacked vitalism for being self contradictory as an unopposed force, he also objected to it being merely an exhaustion of matter.[140] Schelling's rejection of vitalism however comes from a classical articulation of vitalism necessitating a rejection of the effect of physics on life as such, a rejection which our formulation here has sought to negate.

Our dark vitalism as inherently spatio-temporal should alleviate Schelling's second objection since his own system sought to articulate a nature between mechanism and teleology or finalism.[141] In this sense we could say that Schelling's nature appears to be partially similar to Bergson's in that both natures start from a kind of absolute and are divided over time. Kielmeyer's thesis that species are a retrogression from a more advanced form fits into this conception of nature as well.[142]

Yet Bergson seems to situate the differences of nature primarily in the mind whereas for Schelling the differences of nature, the teeming darkness of the absolute is spread over time in an empirical sense.[143] The One of nature must not however be taken to be an ideal form nor must it be seen as a kind of perfect totality of the cosmos. The One must be taken as an obscurity, as the fundamentally unstable beginning of all the processes and entities of the universe. We will address the metaphysical details of this One in the following chapter, for now it is the darkness surrounding the One (that awful absolute) also being the darkness of our dark vitalism which I will tie to the biological horror of the extragalactic Tyranids.

In his text *Difference and Repetition* (a text far too dense to fully explicate here) Gilles Deleuze mentions a dark precursor as something that exists prior to all differences, differences which, for Deleuze, exist prior to identity, prior to sameness.[144] In Iain Hamilton Grant's "The Chemistry of Darkness" Grant points to this darkness of Deleuze and ties it to the dark absolute of Schelling. This Darkness which Hegel and Schlegel ridiculed as too obscure. Nature, for Schelling, is always at least partially buried in "eternal darkness."[145] We could also mention Bergson's dark fringe, of a certain film of darkness surrounding our thinking in relation to evolution where our thinking is around a surface from which the unpredictable springs up and never grasps the internal generative nature of evolution, of nature.[146]

This darkness is not merely an obfuscation but an ongoing challenge to the capacities of thought to think life. Dark vitalism is an alternative to Bergson's combination of idealism and vitalism and a more realistic take on Schelling's marriage of materialism (or mechanism) with vitalism.[147] Dark vitalism accepts a reality that is fundamentally comprised of forces and processes but does not attempt to make this contingency or process-dominated reality something that is immediately thinkable, or understandable within the limits of reason alone. Dark Vitalism then, is a strange combination of realism and vitalism.

The troubled relation of thinking and nature is played out through the relation of the interior and the exterior. As Iain Hamilton Grant writes: "The Idea is external to the thought that has it, the thought is external to the thinker that has it, the thinker is external to the nature that produces both the thinker and the thought and the Idea."[148] For Grant, exteriority is of far more interest than interiority, of the feeling of forms of stratification rather than the fact of stratification itself.[149] Furthermore, thinking can never recount all the details of its production since the accidental nature of time makes this impossible. But, as we saw in the first chapter, interiority cannot be equated with thought but must grapple with the explosion of life itself from the smallest components. Yet a certain darkness hangs over the possibility of life, it surrounds the difference between the inorganic and the organic. This darkness can be aligned with that of the indiscernability of matter and the material make up life itself.

Evolution is not only the stretching of our thinking, to absorb the components and capacity of the ooze of life but also the recognition that thought is only one outcome, one strata of nature itself and not the necessary end of nature's work-towards-life. Whether life comes from elsewhere as a trans-galactic spore, or whether life's individual configurations on separate worlds always lead to similar results, this does not account for the feedback of space and other forms of existence both organic and inorganic, on how we think life and how thinking life emerges or fails to emerge from ponds of swirling muck.

The teeming biological, if beginning from a unity and moving outwards, dividing into ever more chaotic and divergent forms creates a creeping abyss of biology, where reason is only one feature amidst a taloned and toothed pandemonium.

Conclusion

Slime Metaphysics?

"Of human life the time is a point, and the substance is in a flux, and the perception dull, and the composition of the whole body subject to putrefaction, and the soul a whirl, and fortune hard to divine, and fame a thing devoid of judgment."
-Marcus Aurelius, *Meditations*

"A: There is no grand scheme of things.
B: If there were a grand scheme of things, the fact – the fact – that we are not equipped to perceive it, either by natural or supernatural means, is a nightmarish obscenity.
C: The very notion of a grand scheme of things is a nightmarish obscenity."
-Thomas Ligotti, *My Work is Not Yet Done*

One of the most peculiar aspects of Sigmund Freud's *Beyond the Pleasure Principle* is his speculative creation of the vesicle. Freud writes that this bit of life functions "in its most simplified possible form as an undifferentiated vesicle of a substance that is susceptible to stimulation" where "the surface turned towards the external world will from its very situation be differentiated and will serve as an organ for receiving stimuli" as a model for organic experience.[150]

Freud's speculative biology is pursued in an attempt to explain the tendency of living organisms to repeat unpleasant acts, a repetition which Freud asserts connects the organism's initial division into internal and external components by a massive shock to a drive towards the inorganic. That is, while the sexual instincts of organisms tend towards life, towards the continuation of life by way of reproduction, this instinct is powerless against the more powerful death drive, the fact that the ultimate aim of all life is death.[151]

Freud's "little fragment of living substance" which is beset on all sides by "the most powerful energies" is in kind no different from human beings.[152] The difference of human being(s) is the reflective nature of our thinking whether intentional (conscious) or indirect (unconscious). This does not save humanity from the ultimately dismal end of all biological forms, from time's hollowing out and softening of life though we may attempt to in the timelessness of the unconscious, in fantasies and dreams and so forth.[153]

Granting Freud's assumption that the fantasmatic bastion of the unconscious resists the ravages of biological time Freud remarks that "What we are left with is the fact that the organism wishes to die only in its own fashion."[154] The drive towards death, towards the (in)organic pools of our humble beginnings runs against the vacuity of the spiritual cosmetics of meaning and purpose. Freud writes: "It may be difficult, too, for many of us, to abandon the belief that there is an instinct towards perfection at work in human beings which has brought them to their present high level of intellectual achievement and ethical sublimation and which they may be expected to watch over their development into supermen."[155]

Freud has no trouble furthering such abandonment. As Ray Brassier writes: "Death, understood as the principle of decontraction driving the contractions of organic life is not a past or future state towards which life tends, but rather the originary *purposelessness* which compels all purposefulness, whether organic or psychological."[156] That is, the originary moment of life's creation can be thought of as the indifference of entropy and the difference of negentropy joined together in a way we have not yet discovered.[157] It is our attempt at discovering this which, for

Brassier, drives our thinking and our acting. The issue here is discerning the pathology of the human organism without reduction to organism as DNA vessel[158] nor externally transcendentalizing the human and shielding it from physical and chemical processes in a fruitless and poetic gesture.

One large question that remains given Brassier's cosmological inscription of the death drive is whether our concept of life requires a substantive rather than purely identitarian definition. Throughout this text we have rejected the classical view that vitalism assumes a substance and yet the category of life in Henry's terms or the way living or lifestyle is often formulated, eschews the very question of substantive life, of questions of life that many thinkers like to avoid given the possible dangerous ramifications of speaking of life itself and not merely life as such. Life, however, cannot be the metacorporeal entity of classical vitalism[159] that is, a trans-species substance, nor can it be a force which only confuses questions of substance. As Freud points out, Weissman's morphological living substance[160] is divided into immortal and mortal parts as we previously discussed in regards to Bergson's statement that individual forms of life are only buds of a deeper process.

Pearson shows that Deleuze is critical of Weissman's divide of soma and germ because the existence of the germ, of the substance of life, implies that there can be a part of life without change, some part of life that is not pure process.[161] But, Weissman did not wish to allow for any sense of internal development of life aside from its species archetype contained in its germinal (immortal) existence.[162] The deep interior of the germ, the reduction of life to the simple vesicle is symbolically recoded in Lacan's adaptation and mutation of Freudian psychoanalysis in the lamella.

The Lamella (literally meaning man-omlette) is "extra-flat" and "moves like an amoeba."[163] As Žižek describes it, this squirmy bit of life is a rogue organ which embodies pure life instinct, the aforementioned life instinct as embodied by sexual reproduction. By embodying this process however, the lamella is precisely that which is left out of sexual reproduction since the negentropy of organisms is ultimately imperfect.[164] The lamella is simultaneously the core, and leftover of, life's productivity and life as a substance. Lacan refers to the lamella as a phantom after birth, as a more primal form of life.[165] As a fragment of immortal life, it is difficult not to see the lamella as some transformation of Weissman's eternal germ.

The lamella is described as "pure surface," as an inverted organ[166] and while embodying the leftover of reproduction it also simultaneously represents the aforementioned death drive, the "uncanny excess of life."[167] However, one cannot help but notice that the undead nature of the lamella seems to be overly ideal and in service to the persistence of human subjects. That is, whereas Freud-Weissman's immortal piece of life was life itself, the germ of life, Žižek-Lacan's is the repetition of life-forms. In this sense Žižek de-nihilizes the death drive as Pearson states that Deleuze accomplishes as well.[168]

It is worth noting that the Žižek chapter quoted from above is entitled 'Lacan as a reader of Alien' – the face hugger functions as the lamella – sacrificing itself to impregnate a goo-trapped victim with a xenomorph. The fantastical xenomorphs, in Žižek's articulation, are representative of the bare and monstrousness of life and yet he says nothing about the actual capacity of the horridness of nature but instead swings the burden of insanity to the mind of human creatures. The activity of all the world (following a Hegelian strand of thought, in terms of absolute spirt, of an ideal driving force of the world) is psychologized, where all substance, whether biological or inorganic is just stuff.

But can we believe that the awfulness (or cosmological indifference) of the generation of life itself is found only in the dull perception of one species naked apes, or is it in life itself?

The question could be put another way; how slimy is psychoanalysis (or for that matter any philosophical form of materialism) willing to be? In his text *Žižek's Ontology*, Adrian Johnston points out Žižek's profound disgust with life stating that he "finds occasions for dwelling upon these powerful feelings of deep-seated revulsion, feelings that sustain an aesthetic omnipresent in his oeuvre."[169]

Johnston points to images throughout Žižek's work of putrid flesh, disgusting life, ugliness and other assorted horrors such as "an obscene mass of raw, palipating slime."[170] Johnston notes that this is more than a personal oddity for Žižek and that it points to a horror inherent to subjective existence. This horror is rooted in the experience of the subject[171] and not organicity itself. The aversion to slime, according to Johnston, is indicative of an obsessional neurosis, a neurosis that Žižek's uses psychoanalysis to critique in Kant's critical analysis.[172] Despite this Johnston argues that Žižek performs the pathologies he diagnoses in others[173] as he follows the spirit of, but comes to different conclusions regarding, the void or meaninglessness of the illusion of immortality overriding the gross materiality of human (and all biological) life.

This may seem to be completely in line with the darkness of dark vitalism, that life is horrible strictly from the perspective of human beings. However the difference is crucial. Žižek's psychoanalytic philosophy does not see a material existence independent of the human subject where here we are asserting one, this being the fundamental difference between materialism and realism. That is, while psychoanalysis appears to be one of the stronger philosophical articulations from the sense stage of thought, from subject-centered thinking, it does not take nature on the whole as a relevant object of thought in any serious regard.

As Johnston himself has noted mankind is trapped in a weak nature.[174] He then goes to dismiss Freud's biologism stating that instead of material nature as disrupted we have "irreducible discord and clashes arise from antagonistic splits embedded in the material foundations of human."[175] and that nature itself is "heterogeneous ensembles of less-then-fully synthesized material beings."[176] The issue becomes of retaining the weight of the drives on humans without sufficiently de-toothing nature, that is of asserting the organic over the vaguely material.

What is imperative in Johnston's account of the drives of psychoanalysis, and what seems perfectly in sync with a strong or non-weak nature, is their temporal dimension. Connecting the drives to Lacan's lamella Johnston writes "Drives often behave as parasites, feeding off the vitality of their biological host in their insatiable quest for enjoyment."[177] While it would seem that drives are unnatural parasites (with the parasitic image bringing the death drive back to its vesicle or germinal roots) that is, psychic constructs, what if the drives were thought of us our own relation to time itself? That is what if the pure energy of the drives, which Freud articulated as a kind of psychical energy (which might be seen as inherently vitalist) were seen as the force of time itself, as it is interpreted by the organism. In this sense drives, following from the One which we introduced at the intro-duction of this text, would be another result of the decomposition of the original cloud of cosmological matter.[178] What more can be said of this One, of a formal name for the results of time and space's explosion over space? How is the oozing juggernaut of time productive in connection to life?[179]

The neo-Platonist thinker Plotinus provides some clue as he, along with other neo-Platonists, formulated a concept of the One as a complete and utter transcendence. Plotinus' One is a non-concept which is known through its effect as power, foundation and location and is as all that is and what is potential, it emanates all existents and holds all possibility. Against Plotinus' transcendent One which borders on the mystical and the god-like, our One is merely the generative material sum as the specu-lative epoch prior to the Big Bang, the source of all things but in a strictly material sense.

In this sense the One is corrupted or degenerate instead of being transcendent, and instead of being eternal and timeless it is merely the step towards time and space, the possibility of change. Iain Hamilton Grant connects Plotinus' One, and his general theory of an energized or spiritualized world as numbers made manifest, to Lorenz Oken's similar use of the zero.[180]

The invocation of such numbers is only an illustration of an originary event which has set in motion the engine of spatio-temporality causing products such as life and, to connect back to Freud, self-aware life which as to comprehend a force of time which appears simultaneously formative and parasitic.

Schelling's use of *Stufenfolge* (or sequence of steps) brings the issue of the One and of the unsure division of the interior and the exterior and the mortal and immortal parts of life to a synthesis. The *Stufenfolge* names the constant stream of becomings which do not follow from a form and merely attempt to repeat it (the One does not emanate itself) but only processes itself as process[181] The *Stufenfolge* are the decomponents of nature, of the original One creating an infinite series of finite beings, of what we experience as nature.[182]

To return to numericity, Oken's zero, as Iain Hamilton Grant points out in "Being and Slime", is the wavering zero, the generator of all slime which thereby asserts that something (materiality, matter etc) is merely the repetition of nothing as an ideal/intensity or as real/extensive and the reason for all.[183] Nothingness is the reason for all, extended and intensive which preempts all thought, all forms of ideation. That is, there is no reason for what is other then it follows from this or that thing which is a result of the decomposition of the One. Or put most simply things do not happen because thought, or spirit, or fate guarantees that they happen, nor does thought, or spirit or fate itself happen (come to be) because it must, it is just that thought, or spirit or fate (or its material effects) can happen over time as the evolution of our planet has shown. Following Grant's use of Oken, time is the ground of all ideation[184] and human beings are merely thinking slime[185] caught in the flow of time, in a parade of nothingness. One could take the mathematical representation of such a cosmosis as follows:

1.00000000000.

Where the 1 is the congealed time space and matter inherently instable, which explodes outwards in to time and space in relation to matter. Existence, which follows, and what philosophy attempts to grasp as "the formal repetition of cosmogony."[186] Our existence is then only a stacking of putrescence, an infusorial mass or protoplasm or an originative but rotten unity.[187] Okenian biological existence then, is merely one of the results of this explosion of filth, as a generative mucus or *Urschleim*, a collection of slime points (a primordial form of life similar but not analogous to Freud's vesicle) which combine to form different constructions of life.[188] Clark Ashton Smith, a sympathetic organism of H.P. Lovecraft, created a horrific manifestation of such slime being with his Ubbo-Sathla:

> "Ubbo-Sathla dwelt in the steaming fens of the newmade Earth: a mass without head or members, spawning the grey, formless efts of the prime and the grisly prototypes of terrene life . . . And all earthly life, it is told, shall go back at last through the great circle of time to Ubbo-Sathla."[189]

Smith further ties this great mother slime to the evolutionary action of life on Earth:

> "There, in the grey beginning of Earth, the formless mass that was Ubbo-Sathla reposed amid the slime and the vapors. Headless, without organs or members, it sloughed from its oozy sides, in a slow, ceaseless wave, the amoebic forms that were the archetypes of earthly life. Horrible it was, if there

had been aught to apprehend the horror; and loathsome, if there had been any to feel loathing."[190] The aforementioned Frederich Kielmeyer suggested that there were five forces of the organism and that one increased as the others decreased – one of which was the secretive – one can imagine Clark's Ubbo-Sathla as a beast with its secretive power beyond all measure.[191]

Here, against Henry's purely affective life, one can see life as a pool of feculence, as that which has been and will be without inherent feeling (without horror and loathing in Clark's quote). The question becomes does the base materialism of life relate to the problem of ethics – a concern which too often than not is the center of contemporary philosophy at the cost of analytical or speculative breadth and depth. An ethics which must take the productivity and product being of nature seriously.

In "Being and Slime" Grant points out that, following Oken, an ethics without a philosophy of nature is a contradiction, a non-thing.[192] The fundamental challenge of Kantian ethics and of subsequent post-modern ethics (following from thinkers such as Emanuel Levinas) is that they set themselves as groundless, as not following from any sort of nature or material substance. This groundlessness is only half -hearted however, as the dominant form of ethics bases itself on an unacknowledged (or celebrated) positing of the importance of human beings.

The obvious problem of connecting ethics to any sort of materiality immediately suggests the possibility of ethics, or more generally human action, determining life. This problem is only legitimate, however, if life is always taken to be life as such and not life itself. That is, a material ethics immediately summons the specters of eugenics, selective breeding racism et cetera because the concept of a natural ethics is construed as coming from a particular form of human (a particular race, religion, etc.) and not from humans as a slimy animal.

Contemporary ethical configurations then would see a material basis for an ethics following from nature as coming from a particular human subject (Nazi, Fascist et cetera) and never humanity as a form of animal.

Where an Okenian ethics should be viewed as an ethics open to forms-of-life regardless of their material appearance, form or function, the philosophically dominant ethics of the day would see such an ethics as determining a particular form of human life as such (that is secretly western, eastern, Christian and so forth) and never following from biology or the base slime of life itself.

How better to pursue such an ethics of nature, of the biological, than to approach the alien again.

The film *District 9* takes the alien, the outsider and the concept of disease thereby unifying two of our previously discussed adventures (the microbial and the supra organic) with the fungal remaining to feast on the remains. The film follows, in faux documentary style, an aspiring employee of a multinational corporation who leads an eviction of a shanty town of aliens in Johannesburg who, twenty years earlier, came to Earth in a barely functioning ship without any leadership hierarchy, starving and helpless. During the eviction the employee, Wikus, is exposed to a biological agent which slowly begins to transform his body but not before causing his teeth and fingernails to fall out, his skin to deform, and features to change and so on.

These body horror or gross-out aspects of *District 9* may be forgiven if the question of the biological itself is in question in relation to life, the question of how biological is our humanity? The ease at which the body is nullified by seen and unseen agents suggests that it is the gestures of living creatures which creates material difference – even if in a material sense the gestures are 'just rubbish' in a material sense. Wikus, after his transformation continues to make presents of rubbish, such as a metal flower, for his wife. Connecting back to the introduction, meaning is not inherent but retroactive, caused by the interconnectedness and effects of rubbish, of dumb biology. Scenes throughout the film which run becoming-the-xeno-subject and sickness together (when the deplorable protagonist Wikus pulls out his dead finger nails, dead teeth and so forth) tie the danger of a material based ethics to the tenuousness of the material itself due to death, disease rot and so on.

Negarestani's already mentioned radical openness comes into play and, in particular, his depiction of it as being open to being butchered. As Negarestani writes: "The blade of radical openness thirsts to butcher economical openness or any openness constructed on the affordability of both the subject and its environment."[193] Or put another way: "Openness emerges as radical butchery from within and without."[194]

The treatment of Wikus' body by himself, by the alien infection and by others illustrates the butchering aspect of openness, and can be seen in particular in the amputation logic which often appears in horror films surrounding alien infection whether parasitic or viral. This amputation logic is in full effect in the film the *Ruins* where the part must be sacrificed for the whole. For quite some time in the film Wikus' body is a piece of future biotechnology, ready for scrapping and extraction and he himself contemplates ridding himself of his alien arm. Again, thinking back to our viroid chapter, we are reminded of the withering of the body by the alien life forms in *Dead Space*.

Returning to the ethical, the fact that the reason that the aliens stopped on earth is left open suggests that what they needed itself was open or obfuscated - fuel, food, general care etc. Something that could not be provided by their advanced technology – something possibly as the result of an accident. This fact is compounded by the aliens' biotechnology, the fact that the biological is wired to the technological and yet what is missing is the odd ethical gesture. Again, regardless of the base material, what is lacking, what is needed by the aliens, is gesture which overlooks both the need for their technology and the difference of their biology.

District 9 underscores the lack of this gesture in its portrayal of the inability of capitalist/multinational entities to understand the ethical (as if this was anything new) since the ethical fails as soon as it tries to become formalized into law. The ethical remains the unformalizable aspect of the connection of two networks. Similarly, the question remains of the exact circumstances of how the aliens ended up on earth, was it accident or some other exterior force? The accident or string of unfortunate circumstances being the counterpart to the unpredictable ethical gesture.

Here we could make an odd connection to the racial paranoia of HP Lovecraft. Lovecraft has a striking passage in one of his letters from when he was living in New York. He writes:

"The organic things—Italo-Semitico-Mongoloid—inhabiting that awful cesspool could not by any stretch of the imagination be called human. They were monstrous and nebulous adumbrations of the pithecanthropoid and amoebal; vaguely moulded from some stinking viscous slime of earth's corruption [...] the degenerate gelatinous fermentation of which they were composed—seem'd to ooze, seep and trickle thro' the gaping cracks in the horrible houses...and I thought of some avenue of Cyclopean and unwholesome vats, crammed to the vomiting-point with gangrenous vileness."[195]

As Michel Houellebecq points out, the particular race Lovecraft was talking about is an impossible one – Lovecraft was generally disgusted by what he saw as non-western modes of life. Lovecraft incorrectly assumed that one form of civilization could save humanity from itself and this was his mistake. Here Lovecraft's indifferentism betrays itself as he cannot be open to the sliminess of life in his existence while his fiction was rife with them, with the interpentrating encounter between odd materials and and purportedly familiar ones. Compare to the following from Lovecraft's tale "Facts Concerning the Late Arthur Jermyn and His Family":

"Life is a hideous thing, and from the background behind what we know of it peer daemoniacal hints of truth which make it sometimes a thousandfold more hideous. Science, already oppressive with its shocking revelations, will perhaps be the ultimate exterminator of our human species — if separate species we be — for its reserve of unguessed horrors could never be borne by mortal brains if loosed upon the world."[196]

The question is that of the human and the non-human, not the European and its other. In Negarestani's *Cyclonopedia* he proposes the possibility, following from Lovecraft's creations, of a Cthulhoid ethics which he defines as "A polytical ethics necessary for replacing or undermining existing planetary politico-economical and religious systems. Cthulhoid Ethics is essential for accelerating the emergence and encounter with the radical Outside. Cthulhoid Ethics can be characterized by the question 'what happens next?' when it is posed by the other side or the radical outsider rather than the human and its faculties."[197] It is important to note as well that Negarestani's spelling of polytics is indicative of an alternate meaning to the common politics, that of a schizoid, hyperactive forming of strategies to degrade and undue its target by opening it to the untenable Outside.[198]

While openness as a political ethical category is no new creation (going back fifty years at least) Negarestani's formulation, as has been previously suggested, makes an important distinction. As we have been deploying openness so far it should be all too clear that Negarestani's openness is one in which invites hacking and butchering or worse. It is one not of being open to X but being open, making oneself fully susceptible to invasion, corruption, contagion and death. It is an ethics that refuses to let an unacknowledged and subjectively human designation of the ethical over-determine life in itself with life as such.

Humans, like any other polyp of living matter, are nothing

but heaps of slime slapped together and shaped by the accidents of time and the context of space. The fact that we have evolved self-consciousness should not guarantee or maintain meaning. Meaning is only ever the final gloss on being which when removed does not then dictate mass suicide nor pure apathy. Such a suggestion would ignore the pathology of human existence, of the mind as a ball of time, that being permeated by space and time we form particular attachments and drives, things that we pursue, construct and so forth without reason or meaning – only as a result of being aware and yet unaware of our own tenuous formation. Tonnesson's statement from the introduction's epigraph that 'Life isn't even Meaningless' is not merely sardonic or misanthropic, but is a critically existential and even ontological truth.

Life is merely life, not to say that it is less meaningful than meaning itself (outside life) but that meaning itself must be negated, rendered in acid. Meaning is additive and here we have set out to subtract it. This may seem to welcome the horrors of bio-metric government aptly considered and critiqued by the philosopher Giorgio Agamben, of being reduced to a genome, a finger print, a retinal scan. But subtracting meaning, reducing ontological life to biological life is only to unbind pathology which seems like a far more useful weapon in combating a structure then meaning, then a meaningful existence or subjectivity in terms of Agamben's form-of-life. Pathology is far harder to measure, dress and maintain then the concept of a meaningful or true life.

Pathology opens the oddness of the accidentality of any creation in time and space thereby spreading a plague of tenuousness across all of existence. This is not to say that 'anything is possible' nor that insanity will save us, but that everything is destructible and the contrary seems possible given a particular utilization and mutilation of time and space. Everything dies. This introduces the tension between inactivity between inaction and action, that things will perish but so will I. The strange temporality is reflected in the symptom, in that particular things in time form our particular pathological trajectory but this trajectory continuously reminds us of its existence.

The issue becomes the interplexing existence of pathological life and slime life in that they both admit our subjectiviation to space and time. That our creation was a fluke and our articulation as civilized beings is just as meaningless. Meaning utilizes time and space (in terms of history, tradition, culture etc.) to deny, or sublate pathology. Any structure (groups, governments, bureaucracies) are merely historical pathologies, a long repetition and validation of a particular pathology which, given its history, seems to have become un-pathological or permanent, useful or meaningful.

The aforementioned being open, being splayed open, then recognizes pathology but does not legitimate structure. We must remain open to the pathological and to life itself (to make possible a Cthuloid ethics). In the epigraph above Ligotti suggests, through negation, that we are subject to a nightmarish obscenity, namely, as I have argued, in that life is drawn and quartered by spatio-temporality. As Lovecraft was known for saying we are merely atoms drifting in a void but following Oken and Grant these formal points, these zeros, are not without their slime just as the human experience of nothingness is not without its slovenly matter, not without the accidental collision of matter that supplants meaning as its birthright.

The material being of humans, and of all life is a slimy one. Slime is the smudge of reality, the remainder and reminder of the fact that things fall apart. The shining path of humanity is only ever the verminous-like trail of our own oozing across time and space – the trace and proof of our complete sliminess through and through. Human existence then is composed of the slime of being conjoined with the mindless and dysfunctional repetitions of pathology.

Slime, in the end, is the proof of cohesion and the hint of its undoing, the evidence that something disgusting happened, some foul thing called life. Something that will fill space till the cosmos burns too low for anything to again cohere, ending only with an ocean of putrescence spilling over into the boundless void of extinction.

Notes

1   Gould, Stephen Jay, (2007) *The Richness of Life: The Essential Stephen Jay Gould*. W.W. Norton) p 280

2   Gould, *The Richness of Life*, p 283

3   Cohen, Jack and Stewart, Ian (2009) "Alien Science" in *Collapse: Philosophical Research and Development* Urbanomic, vol. 5, p 249-250

4   Johnson, Steven, (2002) E*mergence*, (Simon and Schuster), p 11

5   Johnson, *Emergence*, p 13

6   Cohen, Jack and Steward, Ian. (1994) *The Collapse of Chaos: Discovering Simplicity in a Complex World*. (Viking Adult) p 232

7   Cohen and Stewart, *Collapse of Chaos*, p 233

8   Ibid. p 240

9   Ibid. p 244

10 Ibid. p 335, p 367

11 Ibid. p 435

12 Brassier, Ray (2001), *Alien Theory: The Decline of Materialism in the Name of Matter*, (Warwick: unpublished doctoral thesis), p 13

13 Marcus, Gary (2009) *Kluge: The Haphazard Evolution of the Human Mind*, (Houghton Mifflin) p 12

14 Cohen and Stewart, "Alien Science" p 234

15 Ibid., p 235

16 Brassier, Ray, (2007) *Nihil Unbound: Enlightenment and Extinction*, (London: Palgrave Macmillilan) p 51

17 Brassier, Ray, Grant, Iain Hamilton, Harman, Graham and Meillassoux, Quentin, (2007)"Speculative Realism", in *Collapse: Philosophical Research and Development*, vol. 3, (Falmouth: Urbanomic), p 334

18 Deleuze, Gilles, and Guattari, Felix, (1994) *What is*

Philosophy?, Columbia University Press, p 213

19 Joshi, S.T. (1990) *H.P. Lovecraft: The Decline of the West*, (Berkley Heights: Wildside Press) p 16

20 Schelling discusses this in *Ideas for a Philosophy of Nature* and *First Outline Towards a Philosophy of Nature.*

21 Gould, *Richness of Life*, p 213

22 Ibid. p 214

23 Ibid. p 215

24 Land, Nick, "Pest Interview with Nick Land," no longer available online

25 Negarestani, Reza, (2008) *Cyclonopedia: Complicity with Anonymous Materials*, (Melbourne: Re.Press) p 199

26 Negarestani, *Cyclonpedia*, p 198

27 Ibid, p 210

28 Harman, Graham, (2009) *Prince of Networks : Bruno Latour and Metaphysics*, (Re.press) p 64

29 Galloway, Alexander and Thacker, Eugene (2007) *The Exploit: A Theory of Networks*, (University of Minnesota Press) p 86

30 Negarestani, Reza (2003) "Death as a Perversion: Openness and Germinal Death," in *CTheory* p 4 available online at http://www.ctheory.net/articles.aspx?id=396

31 Negarestani, "Death as a Perversion", p 8

32 Ibid. p 7

33 Thacker, Eugene (2005) "Biophilosophy for the 21st Century", in Ctheory, p 2 available online at http://www.ctheory.net/articles.aspx?id=472

34 Thacker, Eugene (2006) "Cryptobiologies," in Artnode vol 6, Universiat Oberta de Catalunya, p 3

35 Galloway and Thacker, *The Exploit*, p 93

36 Ibid. p 94-95

37 Thacker, "Cryptobiologies," p 5

38 Thacker, Eugene (2008) 'Nine Disputations on Horror,' *Collapse: Philosophical Research and Development* vol. 4,

(Urbanomic) p 67

39   Thacker, "Nine Disputations", p 81

40   Thacker, Eugene (2004) "Living Dead Networks", in *Fibreculture* Journal Issue 4, Online Publication, p 1

41   Negarestani, Reza Militarization of Peace, *Collapse: Philosophical Research and Development* vol 1, p 64

42   Thacker, Eugene "Biophilosophy for the 21st Century", p 3

43   Ibid., p 4

44   Pearson, Keith Ansell, (1999) *Germinal Life: The Difference and Repetition of Deleuze*, (Routledge) p 188

45   Pearson, *Germinal Life*, p 10-11

46   Pearson, *Germinal Life*, p 11

47   Pearson, *Germinal Life*, p 12-13

48   Pearson, *Germinal Life*, p 170

49   Merleau-Ponty, Maurice (2003) *Nature: Course Notes from the College de France*, (Northwestern University Press) p 170

50   Thacker, 'Nine Disputations,' p 87

51   Thacker, 'Nine Disputations, p 87-88

52   Ibid. p 91

53   Ligotti, Thomas (1994)"The Shadow at the Bottom of the World," in *Grimscribe*, (Jove Books) p 225

54   Rofle, R.T. and Rolfe, F.W. (1974) *The Romance of the Fungus World*, (Dover Publications) p 3

55   Ibid. p 5

56   Ibid. p 79

57   Ibid. p 116-117

58   Ibid. p 23

59   Vandermeer, Jeff (2006) *Shriek: An Afterword*, (Tor Books) p 62-63

60   Ligotti, Thomas (2008) "The Bungalow House," in *Teatro Grottesco*, (Virgin Books) p 203

61   Ligotti, Thomas "Severini," in *Teatro Grottesco*, (Virgin Books) p 231

62   Ibid.

63 Ibid.

64 Ibid. p 239

65 Ibid.

66 Ibid. 242

67 Ibid.

68 Weinbaum, Stanley (1935) "Parasite Planet" available online at http://gutenberg.net.au/ebooks06/0601211h.html, accessed 6/1/2010, unpaginated

69 Weinbaum, "Parasite Planet" unpaginated

70 Ibid.

71 Weinbaum, Stanley (1935) "The Lotus Eaters" available online at http://gutenberg.net.au/ebooks06/0601231h.html, unpaginated

72 Rolfe, p 19

73 Rolfe, p 21

74 Rolfe, 40-42

75 Negarestani, *Cyclonopedia*, p 94

76 Bergson, Henri (1998) *Creative Evolution*, (Dover) p 128

77 Rolfe and Rolfe, p 15

78 Hodgson, William Hope "A Voice in the Night," available online at http://gaslight.mtroyal.ca/voicenig.htm. Accessed Nov, 2011 unpaginated

79 Lovecraft, HP (2008) "Nyralhotep", in *H.P. Lovecraft The Fiction Complete and Unabridged*, (New York: Barnes and Noble) p 123

80 Lovecraft, HP (2008) "The Dream Quest of Unknown Kadath" in *H.P. Lovecraft The Fiction Complete and Unabridged*, (New York: Barnes and Noble) p 410

81 Houellebecq, Michel, (2005) *Against the World, H.P. Against Life* (McSweeny's) p 67

82 Lovecraft, HP (2009) "The Fungi from Yoggoth" available online at http://www.hplovecraft.com/writings/texts/poetry/p289.asp. Accessed November, 2011.

83 Ibid.

84   Lovecraft, HP "The Dream Quest of Unknown Kadath," p 411

85   Clark Ashton Smith, (2006) 'The Tale of Samptra Zeiros,' available online at http://www.eldritchdark.com /writings/short-stories/208/the-tale-of-satampra-zeiros, Accessed November, 2011.

86   Houellebecq, Michel in *Collapse: Philosophical Research and Development* vol. 4, 174

87   Rolfe, *Romance*, p 18

88   Negarestani, *Cyclonopedia*, p 182

89   Rolfe, *Romance*, p 2

90   Rolfe, *Romance*, p 290

91   Negarestani, *Cyclonopedia*, p 228

92   Lovecraft, HP 'At the Mountains of Madness,' in *H.P. Lovecraft The Fiction Complete and Unabridged*, (New York: Barnes and Noble, 2008), p 802

93   Gascoigne, Marc and Jones, Andy (2001) (ed) *Dark Imperium*, (Black Library) p 272

94   HP Lovecraft quoted in ST Joshi, *Decline of the West*, p 33

95   Richards, Robert. (2002) *The Romantic Conception of Life: Science and Philosophy in the Age of Goethe.* (University of Chicago Press) p 248

96   Gould, Stephen Jay, *The Richness of Life*, p 373

97   Ian Grant, *Philosophies of Nature After Schelling*, p 121

98   Ibid, p 135

99   Houellebecq, *Against the World, Against Life*, p 33

100 Joshi, S.T., (1990) *H.P. Lovecraft: Decline of the West*, (Borgo Press) p 13

101 Joshi, *Decline of the West*, p 5, 11

102 Joshi, *Decline of the West*, p 84-85

103 Bergson, *Creative Evolution*, p 26-27

104 Joshi, *Decline of the West*, p 89

105 HP Lovecraft, (2008) "The Unnameable," in *H.P. Lovecraft The Fiction Complete and Unabridged*, (New York: Barnes and

Noble), p 260

106 Ibid.

107 Kelly, Phil, and Chambers, Andy, (2004) *Codex: Tyranids*, (Games Workshop) p 2

108 Lovecraft, H.P. "At the Mountains of Madness," p 771

109 *Codex: Tyranids*, p 43

110 *Codex: Tyranids*, p 4

111 Bergson, *Creative Evolution*, p 138-139

112 *Codex: Tyranids*, p 4

113 Grant, Iain. (2008) "Being and Slime: The Mathematics of Protoplasm in Lorenz Oken's 'Physio-Philosophy'" in *Collapse:Philosophical Research and Development* vol 4. Urbanomic, p 307

114 Jack Cohen and Ian Stewart, 'Alien Science,' in *Collapse* vol 5, p 278

115 Ibid. p 279

116 Ibid. p 281

117 Schelling, F.W.J. (1995) *Ideas for a Philosophy of Nature.* trans. Errol Harris and Peter Heath. Cambridge University Press., p 36

118 Ibid. 43

119 Ibid. 54

120 Richards, *Romantic Conception of Life*, p 133

121 Schelling, *Ideas for a Philosophy of Nature*, p 273

122 Fahy, Warren, (2009) *Fragment,* (Delacorte Press) p 70. Thanks to Katie Kohn for pointing out this work to me.

123 *Fragment*, p 250

124 *Fragment*, p 60

125 *Fragment*, p 211

126 *Fragment*, p 281

127 *Fragment*, p 283

128 Schelling, F.W.J. (2004) *First Outline of a System of the Philosophy of Nature.* Albany: State University of New York Press, p198

129 Ibid. p 194

130 Schelling, FWJ, (2007)*The Grounding of Positive Philosophy*, (Albany: State University of New York Press), p 93

131 Richards, *The Romantic Conception of Life*, p 138

132 Ibid.

133 Grant, *Philosophies of Nature after Schelling*, p 119

134 Ibid. p 125

135 Richards, *The Romantic Conception of Life*, p 143

136 Ibid. p 145

137 Grant, *Philosophies of Nature after Schelling*, p126

138 Ibid. p 134

139 Ibid. p 136-138

140 Ibid. p 99-104

141 Richards, *The Romantic Conception of Life*, p 162

142 Ibid. p 248

143 Ibid. p 185-186

144 Deleuze, Giles, (1994) *Difference and Repetition* , trans. Paul Patton, (Columbia University Press), p 119

145 Schelling, *First Outline*, p 98

146 Bergson, *Creative Evolution*, p 46-47

147 Richards, *Romantic Conception*, p 292-294

148 Grant et all, *Collapse* vol. 3, p 339

149 Grant et all, *Collapse* vol. 3, p 340

150 Freud, Sigmund (1990) *Beyond the Pleasure Principle*, (W.W. Norton) p 28-29

151 Freud, *Beyond the Pleasure Principle*, p 146

152 Freud, *Beyond*, p 30

153 Freud, *Beyond*, p 31-32

154 Freud, *Beyond*, p 47

155 Freud, *Beyond*, p 50

156 Ray Brassier, *Nihil Unbound*, p 236

157 Brassier, *Nihil Unbound*, p 238

158 Cohen and Stewart, *Collapse of Chaos*, p 308-309

159 Galloway and Thacker, *The Exploit*, p 80

160 Freud, Beyond, p 54

161 Pearson, *Germinal Life*, p 116

162 Pearson, *Germinal Life*, p 6-7

163 Žižek, Slavoj, (2006) *How to Read Lacan*, *(W.W. Norton)*, p 61

164 Ibid.

165 Lacan, Jacques, (2006) "Position of the Unconscious," in *Ecrits*, trans. Bruce Fink (W.W. Norton) p 717

166 Ibid, 718

167 Žižek, *How to Read Lacan*, p 62

168 Pearson, *Germinal Life*, p. 10-11

169 Johnston, Adrian (2008) *Žižek's Ontology: A Transcendental Materialist Theory of Subjectivity*, (Evanston: Northwestern University Press), p 23-24

170 Johnston, *Žižek's Ontology*, p 24

171 Ibid.

172 Ibid. p 22-23

173 Ibid. p 24

174 Johnston, Adrian, (2008) "Conflicted Matter: Jacques Lacan and the Challenge of SecularizingMaterialism," Pli: The Warwick Journal of Philosophy, vol. 19 (Warwick University) p 166

175 Ibid. p 173

176 Ibid. p 187

177 Johnston, Adrian, (2005) *Time Driven: Metapsychology and the Splitting of the Drive*, (Northwestern University Press), p 166

178 Johnston, Adrian, *Time Driven*, p 196

179 Grant, "Being and Slime," in Collapse vol 4, p 291

180 Iain Grant, "Philosophy Become Genetic," in *The New Schelling*, p 145

181 Grant, *Philosophies of Nature after Schelling*, p 148

182 Ibid.

183 Grant, "Being and Slime", p 302

184 Ibid. p 321

185 Ibid. p 305

186 Ibid. p 321

187 Ibid. p 295

188 Grant, *Philosophies of Nature after Schelling*, p 130

189 Smith, Clark Ashton, (2009) "Ubbo-Sathla," available online at http://www.eldritchdark.com/writings/short-stories/224/ubbo-sathla. Acessed Nov, 2011 Unpaginated.

190 Ibid.

191 Richards, *Romantic Conception of Life*, p 243-244

192 Grant, "Being and Slime," p 287-289

193 Negarestani, *Cyclonopedia*, p 197

194 Ibid. p 199

195 Houellebecq, Michel *Against the World, Against Life*, p 106-107

196 HP Lovecraft, "The Facts Concerning..." in HP Lovecraft, The Complete Tales, p 102

197 Negarestani, *Cyclonopedia*, p 238

198 Negarestani, *Cyclonopedia*, p 242

zero
books

Contemporary culture has eliminated both the concept of the public and the figure of the intellectual. Former public spaces – both physical and cultural – are now either derelict or colonized by advertising. A cretinous anti-intellectualism presides, cheerled by expensively educated hacks in the pay of multinational corporations who reassure their bored readers that there is no need to rouse themselves from their interpassive stupor. The informal censorship internalized and propagated by the cultural workers of late capitalism generates a banal conformity that the propaganda chiefs of Stalinism could only ever have dreamt of imposing. Zer0 Books knows that another kind of discourse – intellectual without being academic, popular without being populist – is not only possible: it is already flourishing, in the regions beyond the striplit malls of so-called mass media and the neurotically bureaucratic halls of the academy. Zer0 is committed to the idea of publishing as a making public of the intellectual. It is convinced that in the unthinking, blandly consensual culture in which we live, critical and engaged theoretical reflection is more important than ever before.